Carl Muller (1935–) is an unusual man. He is no academic; kicked out of three schools, he never went to university and served in the Royal Ceylon Navy, the Ceylon Army and the Port of Colombo as a pilot station signalman. In advertising briefly, he was also involved in the travel trade, and donned the robes of an entertainer. A pianist and a journalist, Carl Muller has a large number of published titles, ranging from poetry to science fiction, under his belt. His 'Burgher novels' earned him special acclaim, especially the first one, *The Jam Fruit Tree*, which won the Gratiaen Memorial Prize, 1993, for the best work of English literature by a Sri Lankan. He has also won the State Literary Award for his historical novel, *Children of the Lion*, the first book in this series.

He lives with his wife, Sortain, in Kandy.

Grandeur of the Lion

CARL MULLER

PENGUIN BOOKS

PENGUIN BOOKS

Published by the Penguin Group

Penguin Books India Pvt. Ltd, 11 Community Centre, Panchsheel Park, New Delhi 110 017, India

Penguin Group (USA) Inc., 375 Hudson Street, New York, New York 10014, USA

Penguin Group (Canada), 90 Eglinton Avenue East, Suite 700, Toronto, Ontario, M4P 2Y3, Canada (a division of Pearson Penguin Canada Inc.)

Penguin Books Ltd, 80 Strand, London WC2R 0RL, England

Penguin Ireland, 25 St Stephen's Green, Dublin 2, Ireland (a division of Penguin Books Ltd)

Penguin Group (Australia), 250 Camberwell Road, Camberwell, Victoria 3124, Australia (a division of Pearson Australia Group Pty Ltd)

Penguin Group (NZ), 67 Apollo Drive, Rosedale, Auckland 0632, New Zealand (a division of Pearson New Zealand Ltd)

Penguin Group (South Africa) (Pty) Ltd, 24 Sturdee Avenue, Rosebank, Johannesburg 2196, South Africa

Penguin Books Ltd, Registered Offices: 80 Strand, London WC2R 0RL, England

First published by Penguin Books India 2012

Copyright © S.O.R. Muller 2012

All rights reserved

10 9 8 7 6 5 4 3 2 1

ISBN 9780143414469

Typeset in Nebraska by InoSoft Systems, Noida
Printed at Replika Press Pvt. Ltd, Sonepat

To my country, and to my giant Indian neighbour
do I dedicate this work
for my love is shared between them.

This world became ablaze by touch of sense afflicted,
Utters its own lament. Whate'er conceit one has
Therein is instability. Becoming other,
Bound to becoming, yet in becoming it rejoices.
Delight therein is Fear, and where it fears is Ill…

…All are impermanent and Ill and doomed to change
In one who sees as it really is by perfect wisdom…

—*Udana 32 (Translated by F.L. Woodward)*

Contents

Silver

On the religio-cultural map of Sri Lanka, one will find a red dot that marks the little village and market square of Ridigama. It lies today, ten miles off Kurunegala on the road to Keppitigala, a quiet, solitary place, nesting passively at the base of the Ridigama rock.

To this place came traders, intent to fill their carts with the ginger that grew in this Malayarata, of which Kurunegala was the main peripheral town. The merchant, Iddampe, was a kindly man. He was well known in the bazaars of the area and the little village markets of the Anuradhapura district where the small home gardens could not grow ginger as successfully as in the foothill regions of the Malayarata. The rhizomes were much in demand in Anuradhapura as well as in the north and east.

Iddampe supplied the ginger, peeled or unpeeled, to his many customers. His little cottage, north-east of Anuradhapura, was, on some days, crowded with helpers, most of them from his wife's family, who would prepare the uncoated ginger for those who wished the tuberous stems peeled.

Iddampe was a very religious man. He would always set apart one cart, which he would lead himself to the many temples, giving the peeled, dry ginger to the monks.

Physicians and ayurvedic practitioners also received ginger at no cost.

'You prepare medicine for the sick,' he would say, 'and how can I take coin from the sick?' Yes, ginger, used in indigestion and fever, was a well-accepted stomachic and aromatic stimulant.

Today, Iddampe and some of his assistants trundled along in their carts. They were in sight of the Ambatthakola cave.[1] 'We will stop here awhile,' he shouted, leaping off the shafts of his cart and clicking his bullock to a halt. 'Let the beasts loose, my brothers. They can graze awhile and we shall stretch our limbs. Ah, that was a long climb, to be sure.'

All around, the low mountain squatted, blurred in a light mist. Only the stark Ridigama rock rose, etched bold and black. The land mounted in waves behind it, densely covered with jungle trees, and below them, the sleepy village. 'Watch the bulls,' he called. 'I go to cut some switches that we will need to jog these lazy creatures along.'

The bulls browsed the thick grass, twitching their sides and swishing away the flies as they munched contentedly. Iddampe took the tiny pebble-strewn path, red and jagged with buried roots and ledges of flint. Having cut a few springy canes, he sat to look upon the sharply dipping terrain, rolling thick grass, jumbles of shrubs and rearing trees. He felt thirsty. When he returned, he found two of the men reclining in the crude hammocks of sackcloth strung under the carts.

'Ho! You sleep,' he shouted, 'and what of the animals? Quickly, lazy ones, one of our bulls have strayed. See, one is missing. Yoke the others. I will find the one that has wandered away.' Much annoyed, he stalked away as the men muttered crossly and shouted to the bullocks.

Rounding the rock, Iddampe paused. He stood before the large cave, a patch of soggy grass where a drip ledge led water into a natural declivity.

Yes, there were the prints of a bull in the brown mud. The cave was enormous. 'Could it be that the wretched animal has gone into it?' he wondered. The exposed roots of trees straggled at the entrance, pythons of ash and sienna, and there rose a large breadfruit tree in which, on a low branch, a green barbet had made its nest and sat, scolding incessantly. Then he gasped. A single breadfruit—but so large: as large as a water pitcher, and its weight had surely dragged low the branch. 'But this is a marvel,' he breathed. 'Such a breadfruit have I never seen—and mature too.' He reached up on tiptoe, tapped the fruit. It gave a firm but hollow sound. 'Yes, well matured. It must be picked and cooked before it rots and goes to waste.'

He gave a little leap and seized the branch on which the fruit hung, dragged on it. The barbet swept up, piping shrilly, then swooped to cling to where its eggs lay. Iddampe smiled. 'Do not worry. When I have taken the fruit, I will release the branch gently.' He would have normally twisted the fruit off at the stem, but today he cut it away with his knife. Milk from the severed stem dripped on his shoulder as he slowly released the branch, then picked up the fruit, turned it over and marvelled at it. 'This must be cut up and cooked now...a good midday meal, enough and too much.'

Carrying the fruit down the track, he found a natural hearth of stone. He quickly stripped kindling from the bushes, then called to the others to bring a large pot and tin plates. 'Some salt too, brothers, and a little turmeric and a pot of water.'

Even as he peeled, cut and dropped the wedges of hard white pulp into the water, he thought, 'So much of this there is. I must first give of what is boiled as alms...but who is there in this place to offer such a meal... and,' he told the others crossly, 'the bull is still missing.'

The wind began to frolic, raising little puffs of dust that seemed to dance between the rocks. To Iddampe, the giving of the first portion of the boiled breadfruit as alms was most important. He was certain that he would court the attention of the *pretas*—those hungry ghosts who would appear quivering, filled with insatiable greed. He looked around anxiously, then his expression changed as he saw, not far away, a small, yet vigorously growing banyan tree. Yes, the deity of the tree would protect him. He took the pot off the fire, laid it firmly upon a cleft of rock and sighed. He turned to his assistants. 'Let us make obeisance to the devata of the Nuga first.[2] See, the sun rides a long way up in the sky. It is mealtime, surely.'

Even as they rose from the cool shade of the banyan, they were startled at the sight of four monks who stood silently, their faces calm, their robes untouched by the quickening wind. Iddampe fell to his knees, then rose with a look of gladness. 'Holy sirs, how pleased I am that you come as you do. And yet, from this spot with the road below, we did not mark your approach.'

The monks were silent. They looked at Iddampe with gentle eyes.

'I, I was doing honour to the tree spirit, holy sirs. It is the mealtime and...and the breadfruit is so large and... and...'

The monks went to the sloping bed of rock. Iddampe was flustered. 'I wished to give first of the fruit as alms. The...the pretas may trouble us...'

Carl Muller

The monks seated themselves on the rock and placed their begging bowls beside them. The boiled breadfruit was yellow, thick and fragrant. Iddampe poked the side of one of his men. 'Fetch a ladle,' he hissed. He went to where the monks sat. 'A large breadfruit did we boil and it is so floury. Boiled in water and with salt and spices, there is some gravy too...taste first of this gravy that is thick and just as floury, holy sirs...' and he quickly filled the alms bowls. The monks gestured their gratitude and rose.

'But you must surely eat of the boiled fruit as well...'

The monks held the bowls of the warm gravy, gave him a sign of blessing and turned away, walking softly down the path. Iddampe sighed. 'Now we shall eat—and then will we find our bull.'

The leaves of the banyan tree rustled and the noon sun touched them with warm fingers. Iddampe took the ladle to the pot. 'Come brothers, let's eat.'

One of his men, Ambatta, put down his plate. 'Wait, wait, the monks return.'

Iddampe stared. They were not the monks who had just walked away, but four others, also silent, their alms bowls empty. He went to them. 'Let us fill your bowls, holy men. We have much to eat and I have called the mealtime.'

They looked at him kindly as he filled their bowls with large pieces of the fruit. One stood, his hand hovering over his bowl. He then walked away, taking the path to the mouth of the cave. The others nodded and walked away.

'Let us eat,' said Ambatta with some impatience. 'Or do we wait for more monks to come?'

'Eat then...there is still so much, so eat your fill and I will do so too.' He looked towards the rise. The monk sat there. It was only when the monk raised food to his mouth that Iddampe also ate. Yes, the breadfruit was most satisfying. He ate with relish and the monk also ate with much satisfaction.

'I'm full,' said one of the men, 'and there's so much more in the pot.'

'Yes. What a fruit this is. As big as a young jak...put what remains into a bag. We cannot let it go waste. I will ask the monk if he wishes more...' As Iddampe stepped up the path, the monk rose and began to climb towards the higher rocks beyond the cave. Iddampe hurried after him. Here lay wilderness and thorn bushes and sharp slivers of stone. Rocks rose like black-shouldered giants. 'Holy one, where go you in this wild place?' Iddampe panted.

The monk raised a hand, pointed to a thick screen of shrub that seemed to crawl high upon the face of rock. 'Go along the path, lay brother,' he said. Iddampe stared. It seemed so unreal that this noontime visitor had actually spoken. 'A path, venerable sir...but...what path is there?'

'Listen well. Your bullock calls. Do you not hear it within that tangle?'

Iddampe nodded. Yes, it had to be his bull...in that thicket, and yes, there was a path. He saw the snapped twigs, the flattened grass of the animal's passage. 'In there?' he asked. There was no reply. The monk had gone.

With an exclamation, Iddampe sped down the slope, calling for a cleaver. Seizing one he said, 'Remain here. See to the animals. I have found our bull!' Swinging the long knife, he raced away while Ambatta shook his head in astonishment.

Slashing his way through the bushes and spiky undergrowth, Iddampe saw before him a blackness that seemed to leap at him. There, against the rock wall, his

6   Carl Muller

bullock stood, munching the young heads of bramble. There was a large, black cavern. It had to be another passage to the Ambatthakola cave, more immense than the entrance beside the breadfruit tree. Stroking the sides of the animal, he peered in, saw glints of light that danced on the inner walls. With a deep breath, gripping the knife, he entered. Yes, the walls seemed to flash, the light moving with the shadows of the thicket outside. His eyes widened. He ran his hands on the walls. Could it be...he struck at a protuberance with his axe and a chunk of rock fell away, revealing an inner skin that glowed white.

'Silver!' he exclaimed. He struck hard, then harder. The rock drew sparks from his axe and at his feet lay a great lump of silver which he picked up with a glad cry. At the entrance he shouted to his bullock and waving his hands willed the creature to move away. 'Hurry, you worthless beast! Don't you know to go back the way you came?' With some difficulty and much shouting, he steered the animal back, turned its head towards the slope. 'Juk! Juk! Go! Go on, stupid creature, go!'

He was breathing hard when he came to the others who had readied for departure. He put the lump of silver into his cart. 'You men go on and collect the ginger, fill the carts as we always do. I must return to the city.'

'But you take one cart away. Our collection will be so much less...'

'It will not matter. Do you see this? Silver! Silver, I tell you. A whole mountain of silver! There, even the cave walls are silver, dressed in rock. I must tell of this to the king.'

One of the men shrugged. 'And what about us? Would it not be better if we filled the carts with this silver instead. Three carts of silver is surely better than...'

'Be quiet! Think you, a holy monk led me to this treasure. Can we take it for ourselves? It is the king who needs wealth such as this. What have you got in your minds, eh? What?'

They watched him go, prodding the bullock to a fast trot, raising a little stream of dust. 'He makes haste. Let us go about our business.'

Ambatta nodded. 'Rich we will never be,' he complained.

The others laughed. 'But ginger we know...silver we don't.'

They guided the wagons to the road, then pushed the oxen to a trot. The ginger needed to be collected before the evening waned.

Duttha Gamani had little time to give audience to the many who came to the palace with their strange tales of treasure. What with the discovery of fields of gold at Accaravitthigama, copper at Tambapittha and precious gems at Sumanavapi, his treasurer and some of his council had complained of the numbers who insisted on telling of rare and costly finds.

'See to it,' he told his treasurer. 'Let a team of officials receive these people, listen to what they have to say. And would it not be better if our queen direct this? Go, say to her that it will be most welcome to us if she would take charge of this. Also, it will be of much satisfaction to the people to be taken into her presence.

And what of the fishermen from Uruvela?[3] Have they also come with some priceless find?'

'We have detained them, lord, that you may see what they have brought.'

At a signal, slaves carried in two large earthen vessels, placed them before the king, bowed low and backed away. The treasurer picked out the most exquisite pearls and chunks of coral, all vermilion, and cast with melting shades of turquoise. Duttha Gamani exclaimed in wonder. He peered into the vessels, took a large pearl to the light, traced a finger over the iridescence of the coral shards. 'And what do these fishermen say?'

'They were casting lines from a belt of sand at the river mouth, great one. The river is low, and much sand lies across the mouth. The sea creeps upon the river when the waters rise and such a good spot gives them many fish. They say how the waters of the river thinned and lay back and the sea rose and the waves crashed upon the sand with unaccustomed force. They ran back, for never had they known such a movement of the sea. With each wave, they say, the sea retreated to a goodly distance, then rolled back and flooded the sand bar. Then, sire, when the waters stilled, the sand and the river bed became as a field of lustrous pebbles. Pearls such as these, and coral, lord, and they hurried to the village and brought men and wagons and litters of thatch. Six wagon loads did they fill, and have brought these to you and await your wishes.'

'Six wagons! Let these men be richly rewarded. Wait, let them return to the river as our royal watchmen, and for these services, henceforth see that they are also paid. Our treasurer must take stock of what has been brought.'

Iddampe fretted in the waiting hall. He wanted to shout his news, show the great lump of silver he carried. Surely the king would be impressed. This was wealth indeed—wealth for the great thupa. When *would* the king see him?

Just then, a hunter strode in. He had left his bow and quiver at the sentry post and his dogs at the gates. Iddampe knew of this man, for his wife brought much ginger each time she came to Anuradhapura. He was puzzled. He knew that this man, Vijith, lived at the edge of the wild country, that his wife prepared many decoctions and medicinal compounds for the people of her village, people who mostly planted rice, gathered fuel wood and made excellent buffalo curd. She always sought out Iddampe for the best ginger he could offer, using the ginger in her many poultices and liniments and for special ointments she made for sufferers of white leprosy.

Leprosy was considered a contagious disease, and sufferers were always sent to live in specially provided wilderness pits. Vijith's woman earned much merit treating the lepers. She would come to the palace each week to collect coins from the monies set aside for the treatment. While she relied very much on ginger, she also prepared special decoctions from the bark, roots, flowers, leaves and fruits of certain plants that grew in the forest.[4]

'Is it you, Vijith? Many miles from your settlement, are you not?'

The hunter smiled. 'Ah, the seller of ginger. Yes, I rode the distance and used the path of every stream so that my dogs would not thirst. But such a wonder have I seen.'

Iddampe clapped him on the shoulder. 'I, too came to tell of a great find, my friend. I told the others to fetch the ginger today. This thing I have found is of utmost worth.'

'Gem flowers!' Vijith said, running a hand through his thick hair. 'Just imagine. Never have I seen such beauty.'

'Gem flowers? What are they?'

Vijith's voice shook as he told of his find. 'It was the singing. Voices that came from nowhere. My dogs must have heard it first, for they stopped and began to whine and some sat and others lay their noses to the ground. Do you know how the jungle shoulders the tank there?'

Iddampe shook his head. He did not like the jungle village where Vijith lived. Pelavapigama[5] was far north. Long ago, the people there had caused the river, the Pali Ara, to be dammed, creating a tank[6] for the crude cultivation of the hunter-village and also for the water that was channelled to the leper pits.

'The dogs would not move, and my horse grew restive. Such singing it was. It came with the wind across the water and then from the small cave on the side of the bund. There is soft earth there and pebbles and dark sand. The boys take worms from this earth for their fish hooks. I went to the cave and what do I see...what did I see?'

Iddampe shook his head.

'Gem flowers! Big, like the flowers of the flax and they had sprung from the earth. Each flower was big. Big like a millstone, I tell you. One so golden in radiance, another like rich blood and one that was blue was as deep-coloured as the water at first light; and yet another so dazzling that it was as a small sun. And the singing filled my head. I was afraid, man. Afraid to approach, but the voices were kind and gentle and I went to the flowers. Real gems! Gems that grew as flowers out of the sand! You should have seen my dogs, inching around on their bellies. I had to come, to ride hard to tell the king. Why am I kept waiting?'

An official entered the little ante chamber. 'Come,' he said to Vijith, 'you will ride with us, show us these gem flowers.'

'That I will. Does the king know of them?'

'The king wishes you to lead us, and if what you say is what you say, much good favour will you receive. And you?' turning to Iddampe, 'you wish to show to the king what you bring?'

Iddampe bowed and held up the sack.

'This is silver! Where did you come upon so large a nugget?'

'Not just this, but a whole mountain. Within the Ambatthakola cave. It was a holy thera who showed me the way to a secret entrance.'

'This must you say to the king...you will wait at the inner gates,' he told Vijith. 'What of your dogs? Will they run with us?'

'That they will if we take the way we came.'

'That is well.' He then led Iddampe to the audience hall.

Silver...No one knew at the time that the mountain of the Ambatthakola cave was also riddled with other caves where arahats lived, unknown, in communion with the devas. They had come unseen upon Iddampe, and had left just as mysteriously. Today, one can reach this cave which is 18 kilometres from the bustling, rock-girt town of Kurunegala, and in doing so, one steps into the days of Duttha Gamani, actually see him carved in stone—a well-formed, almost graceful figure, slim-waisted and strong-shouldered.

Duttha Gamani was pleased. More pleased to know of the thera who had pointed Iddampe to the cave of silver. He had his advisers make a hurried survey, declare the extent of the deposit. 'We will take all that is necessary and then

Carl Muller

must we make it a place of special veneration.' He called on the arahat Indragupta who was the spiritual adviser to the palace. 'A silver vihara must we make of the cave of silver, holy one; and ever must we praise the Lord of the World. No, not one but many viharas, for that is a holy mountain indeed.'

'It is a good intent, O king, but this gift of the devas must we now use. Let the work on the great thupa now begin.'

Vihara Maha Devi urged her son to leave all else. 'We will build there the viharas as you wish, but surely much else needs to be done there first. The roads must be cleared and broadened. Steps must we cut up the mountain and the cave must first be relieved of its silver, then it must be enlarged. You say right. There must be other viharas too; one where the breadfruit was plucked and of which the arahats ate, and another to look upon the others as a sentinel.'

Duttha Gamani nodded. 'All this will take long, our mother.'

'Yes. This is why we shall wait. Let us commence the major work for which all this has been given. Can we ask the devas to wait while we build elsewhere?'

'And surely it was a *vanaprastha*[7] who gave to us this mountain of silver. Such powers do these ascetics command. Are they not holy monks who have achieved the perfect expansion of their spiritual selves?'

'Honour them we shall…but think, they gave this silver that the great thupa be built. Is this not what they wish you to now do?'

Duttha Gamani gave a faint smile. 'Always you think better than I. We will fulfil the prophecy and then turn our attention to so much else that demands our attention. The cave must be a vihara and in it must we place the finest statue of the Conqueror that all may know of his existence in this and all worlds.'

'Well said indeed. Many such arahats reside in caves, in secret places. So many do come and go in the jungle fastness around the Missaka mountain[8] and Samankuta[9] and Sonnagiri.[10] Such extraordinary beings they are. They sleep on the bare ground and refrain from all worldly pursuits.'

'And we can do naught but do them honour. They seek such austerity that truly, we feel helpless.'

Vihara Maha Devi's face softened. She looked affectionately at her son who, with age, was so regal a figure. This find of silver excited her. She was well aware of the riches of the island: pearls and coral from Uruvela, precious stones in the foothills, the mountains; copper, gold, chanks, mica, iron ore...but silver...why, Ambatthakola was the only place of silver now known. And yet, the silversmiths did so much in the city and in their villages: artificial trees, bells, book clasps and covers, bowls, ladles, girdles, parasol handles, the fittings on royal palanquins, moon emblems, vases, lamps, festoons, even toothpicks and ear spoons. Yes, much silver would her son need and like all else, much silver had been miraculously given. There had always been a great trade in silver, and now, a mountain of silver had been given to her son.

Truly, the devas smiled upon him and upon all the land.

Ratnavalli

IT IS TIME TO CONSIDER THE POWER AND THE POSITION OF THE tree spirits who have played so vital a part in the lives of the people of ancient Lanka.

Anuradhapura, city of the lion, had many powerful sylvan deities. As this story rolls on and when it does end, we will know that ninety-three Sinhalese kings reigned in all glory and eleven Damila usurpers also had their seats of government. In this city were raised buildings of such great magnitude—monuments that were as enduring and as historically important as those of the Incas and the Pharaohs.

While it has been accepted that the name, Anuradhapura, derives from the city of the two Anuraddhas, and additionally from the constellation Anura, under which the city was founded, there are many other theories. Major Forbes[11] insisted that the city was so called because it had ninety kings.[12] An inscription of the fifteenth century[13] called the city Anurai, and most happily, the *Maha Bodhi Vamsa* refers to it as *Anurodhijana*—the city and abode of contented, happy people. And how, you would ask, would there be such happy people unless the gods they bowed to were not also as happy and content?

Every king did all that could be done to beautify, to build. We have seen how Panduk Abhaya laid out four suburbs, built the Abhaya tank,[14] a public cemetery, a place of execution, villages for the huntsmen, even for the 500 *chandalas*[15] and dwellings for the scions of different sects. There was, even then, the outer city, the Mahameghavana Gardens, the Nandana Gardens and the inner citadel.[16]

Even today, the city bristles with a grandeur one sees in the great works, and especially in the construction of dagabas or stupas. Such enormous structures were they. Even as Duttha Gamani readied to build the greatest of all, we turn to an old manuscript, the *Vaijyayanta* that tells us of the methods of construction—methods carefully followed and that too, so feverishly that Anuradhapura, down the centuries to this day, and for all the centuries to come, will shout to the world of the religious edifices it holds and in which it was near saturated.

The *Vaijyayanta* tells us in two verses, of the shapes of the dagabas:

Thupesa tharam krita panca bhagam
Gunan pamanantribhga tungam
Ganthakara dhanyakam
Bubbulakara dhanyakam
Padmakarambala shat vidam

Having divided the width of the thupa into five parts, three parts of the latter is considered to be the height of the thupa.
The six kinds of thupas are named as bell-shaped, pot-shaped, bubble-shaped, paddy-shaped, lotus shaped and fruit-shaped.

Further stanzas say:

Thupesu taram krita panca bhagam
Gunan pamanan catuvisa bhagam

Trimala pancarddhaka garbham ashtam
Catussarakoshta yugardha yugman
Shastanta kuntam punardha chatram
Vadanticatah munihih puranam

Having divided the width of the thupa into five parts,
the length of the same is divided into twenty-four parts;
for three storeys, five-and-a-half; the tomb, eight.
To the four-sided godlings' enclosure[17] two-an-a-half,
for the entire spire, the remaining six and a further half
for the Chatta.[18]

As is seen, the ancient sages prescribed the proportions, and this was carefully followed. But along with the buildings, it was also seen how carefully the monarchs of the land guarded and nurtured the trees, the great rocks, the waterways and the forests. Let it also be said that from earliest times, the Sinhalese believed in the creation myths of the Hindus, but with some modifications. First, as has been told, a great rain destroyed the world that had been created by Brahma. Then came fire that was also a destructive force, and with the fire a great darkness. But the world and the stars were born again and there was the sun, the moon, the oceans and a new world as it was before.[19] The story then tells of the coming of plant life, of creepers, crops of paddy and animals.[20]

With this 'groundwork' came the beings of the universe. The *Pujavaliya* lists these as the devas, Brahma, the Nagas, Suparnas, Garudas, Ghandarvas, Yakshas, Rakshasas, Ushna-Valakhas, Agra-Valakhas, Sita-Valakhas, Vata-Valakhas and Vassa-Valakhas, Siddhas, Vidyakaras and other divine hosts. There are also eight hells listed and they are called Sanjiva, Kalasutraya, Sanghataya, Raurava, Maha-Raurava, Tapa, Pratapa and Avici. Yet another place of torment, said to be a region of flame and molten metal, is known as Lokumbu.[21]

Other mythical beings were celestial musicians and magicians, demons and evil entities. There are many Sinhalese today who still believe (and usually when they are sorely tried) that they are still under the curse of Kuveni. In *Children of the Lion*, it was told how Vijaya was helped by a female demon—a yakshini—named Kuveni. Vijaya made a solemn oath to Kuveni and agreed that he would never wed another princess:

> Even if the seeds sown wither, the land become water-logged, goods, crops and seeds become barren, I shall not leave you and take another queen.[22]

But Vijaya was not true to his word and Kuveni was banished. Many are the stories of the yakshini's anger and agony. In the *Sihaba Asna*, we are told of how her curse made Vijaya childless and how she came to him in his dreams as a leopard, bursting through the doors of his chamber, tongue pointed at his heart. It was the god Sakra who intervened, saved Vijaya. Kuveni did not leave Panduvasdeva alone either. One text says that to him also she appeared as a terrible leopard, two-gav long, with a diamond-shaped tongue that could pierce seven doors.[23] Panduvasdeva was also unable to sire children and was afflicted with asthma, diabetes, emaciation and subject to virulent fevers, coughs and burning sensations.

With such evil that could manifest itself at the drop of a crown, the Sihala also accepted the class of spirits they knew to be devas and devatas, many of whom were of a kindly and benevolent disposition. They could be found on mountain peaks, in forest trees, among creepers and even between blades of grass. Sylvan deities were honoured with offerings of food and flowers. These tree spirits exercised their powers for the good of mankind and assisted, warned of and intervened in times of mortal danger. Kiriella Gnanawimala Thera tells us that no lordly trees were cut for fear that the beneficent deity would leave the vicinity.[24] It is also believed that forest deities actually weep when a tree spirit is forced to leave its abode.[25]

Duttha Gamani had spent tireless days in the launching of his great work; and he was impatient. 'Look you,' he said to his councillors. 'It must be on the full moon days of Vesakha[26] that the work must begin. On the night of the appearance of the Visakha stars. Then, in commencement, we must take away the stone pillar of the prophecy. Will the tree devata in that spot heed our pleas?'

His councillors stroked their beards thoughtfully. They knew that the actual relationship between the devas and the tree was of a mystical character, and yet was this not an acceptance of the Sihala drawn from the Hindu repugnance towards the destruction of life in any form? It was always accepted that in any work, any act of building, any architectural enterprise, the nature spirits who may be offended or injured by such work must be propitiated. Behind this, as is seen, was the Hindu sympathy for everything that had life, and apart from the life of the tree itself, the life it harbours. Vasu made a strong claim to this fact:

> A true Hindu would not heedlessly injure the slightest object that has life. A tree is as much a manifestation of the divine wisdom and power as the man himself, and the devas engaged in the building up of a flower, love the

work with as much fond regard as the artist who paints its picture, loves the semblance. The man who, through thoughtlessness or ignorance, injures these divine works, incurs the anger and ill will of these elemental workers. Therefore, a Hindu, in plucking a flower or cutting a twig, prays to the Supreme and asks permission of the industrious ones who have made it. By the very fact that he recognises their labour and appreciates their actions, he propitiates these sylvan devas and gets their goodwill and blessing.[27]

'Lord king,' a councillor said, 'there is no doubt that a most powerful devata dwells there, for many a time has a face been seen among the branches. It is the face of a woman, full grown, the people say, and the sun touches her tresses, and the people spread flowers upon the ground.'

'Assuredly, this devata lives within the tree, great one,' said another, 'and would it not be of necessity that the king ask if she would yield her home so that the great dagaba be built there?'

Duttha Gamani pursed his lips, looked around the chamber. 'Is it that we must go to this devata and tell her of our needs?'

'Most certainly, sire, for we feel the goddess will heed none but thee.'

'And this tree...is it hollow, do you think?'

'No, lord, of that we are certain. It would be unthinkable to fell a tree of hollow trunk, for naught but evil would arise.'

Duttha Gamani nodded. Too well he knew of the many attributes of trees.[28] 'Very well, summon the wise ones that we may prepare our visit. Is it known how we should address this devata?'

'No, but it is said that her occupation of this tree is but recent. People say that her presence was made known even as you led your men to the Ritigala Fort.'

'Surely she came here to await your triumph, lord.'

Duttha Gamani gave a puzzled frown. Why would a sylvan deity come to inhabit a tree at the site of the great thupa? Surely must the spirit have known that the site would be cleared for building. 'We shall go to this tree. It intrigues us that such a devata should take residence there.'

The astrologers and wise men outlined the rituals that had to be performed before the king made approach. It was a mellow evening with a sky that held the soft hue of a newly ripening cherry. At the tree, offerings of flowers were made together with sandal paste and the wise men chanted in quavering voices of their love for the tree and of all other trees where surely, they intoned, others of the devata's family resided. They then cleaned the dead leaves and twigs around the roots and set pots of clear water and sandal milk at the four corners. Clasping hands, they made their plea: 'O deva, much honour do we do thee. We have made this place pleasant and purified it in a manner you would surely approve of...'

The breeze stirred the leaves of the top-most branches, and the gold of the evening turned a dusky bronze. That tinkling sound could not have been made by the light wisps of air that gave life to the leaves. They looked up expectantly. A voice seemed to float over them—a voice of sweetness, light, yet so sharp-toned that each syllable was as a pluck of a lute string. 'Let your labours cease, O wise ones, for here do I await the coming of the king. It will please me much to see him before me before this night is over and the warm day returns. Go now, for I await the coming of yet another in the hours of darkness.'

The astrologers stepped back, mumbling among themselves. They had a ritual to complete and did not know if they could. The spirit of the tree wished them away.

'But we must take of this tree a branch…take it to the other tree we have cleansed, and implore the devata to occupy that tree,' one said. There was concern in his voice.

'What if this is a trick—a ruse that the devata may remain here?' another whispered.

The branches shook. 'Go!' the voice said, and there was a hint of severity in it. 'No more need you labour here.'

They backed away. In the gathering gloom a dog barked and they heard the quarrelling of bats along the line of trees that skirted the distant wall. Even as they hurried off, they heard that tinkling laugh again. What would they tell the king?

It was an ordered ritual. All they had to do was prepare another tree, take a branch from the first tree, place it beneath the new tree. They would then, with silver-tipped rods, draw the *atamagala*—the eight auspicious objects: the lion, bull, elephant, water pot, fan, flag, chank and lamp. It was only then that they could call out to the deva of the tree: 'I pray thee, deva, go to the new tree and give thine own to me.'

This procedure, as we know, is told of in the *Bhadda Sala Jataka*, where the story of the ruler of Benares is beautifully rendered. The writer has found among the Jataka tales an exceptional fount of marvelous literature, and readers will find *The Jatakas* edited by E.B. Cromwell (1895–1907) a treasure indeed. The tale of the *Bhadda Sala Jataka*, which is found in Volume IV of Cromwell's rendition, is truly splendid and bears repetition:

In Benares, ruling well and wisely and observing the Ten Duties of a monarch, was Brahmadatta, and one day he thought upon how he could surpass all the other kings of India. And the thought came to him that all these other kings had royal buildings of many columns. 'What if we would cause to be built a magnificent palace, and built so that it would be supported by a single column? Will not this make us unique?'

He then summoned his craftsmen. 'Build us a palace glorious to behold,' he said, 'and let it be supported by a single pillar.'

The craftsmen went to the forest. Such a task was this. Surely they needed a tree of great girth and strength. But soon they found such a tree, sturdy of aspect and they considered it for long. 'How will we remove such a tree to the city? The road is broken and rough and this tree is too huge to be moved after it is felled.'

They returned to the king, explained their predicament, and the king frowned. 'You must bring hither this tree somehow.' But the craftsmen knew this could not be done. 'It is impossible, great one. It cannot be done anyhow or somehow.'

The king made an impatient gesture. 'Very well, leave that tree to grow in the wilderness. Seek ye in the royal park. There must be fitting trees there.'

There, in the king's park, stood a lordly *sal*[29] that rose straight and splendid. This tree was worshipped by the people of the city and the villages. Even the royal family paid it homage for it was the dwelling of a kindly deva. The craftsmen nodded among themselves. This tree would make that single pillar. They went to the king, who nodded. 'Well, since the tree has been found and is, as you say, suitable, go ye now and fell it.'

The craftsmen knew that they would have to appease the deva. They took scented garlands, silken cords, flowers and votive lamps. At the tree, they hung the garlands on five branches and tied the silk cords around the trunk, fastening to them large clusters of flowers. They lit the lamps, placing them around in the four directions. In the tree, the spirit watched, silent. The leading craftsman then made a gesture of obeisance and said, 'On the seventh day from this day will we fell this tree. This we do on the king's command. We pray that the deva who dwells here depart to another tree, for trees such as this are there elsewhere. May no blame come upon us.'

In the tree, the deva was given to much sorrow. Even as the the craftsmen left, he thought of how his home would be destroyed. 'When my home, my life's habitation is destroyed, I will surely perish, and even as I fall, will I not bring down the other trees of this sal grove. And in these other trees dwell many of my kindred. They too will die as I do.'

Resolving to save the other devas in the grove, he left the tree in the middle hours of the night, appeared in the bed chamber of the king, glowing and filling the room with rays of gold. Hovering at the king's head, he began to moan his plight.

King Brahmadatta awoke and trembled at the unearthly sight. Fearfully, he shielded his eyes and in a hoarse voice asked, 'Who art thou? What god floats beside my pillow, garbed as an angel, and why do you weep so?'

The deva looked down on the king with melting eyes. 'In thy realm, O king, do not your people call me the tree of good fortune? Know you how long I have stood, first in one tree and then in another, and now in the tree of thy park? For sixty thousand years in the great trees of my habitation have I brought good fortune to all, and the people love and worship me. And this is why so many houses have been built, and great palaces too, yet none have done me wrong, sought my home. Yet, do you seek to destroy me, O king. Rather must you honour me as all others have done and still do.'

The king sat up, looked earnestly at the deva. 'But how will we build? Our craftsmen say that your tree has a fine trunk, thick and strong and great of girth. How else can we build a palace that can stand on one pillar?'

'Then you have set yourself to destroy me. I cannot ask you not to do so, but in doing so be it in such a way that my pain will not be grievous. Cut me limb from limb, O king. Cut first my top-most branches, cut me small, piecemeal, then do you cut the middle and then at my roots. Fell me so I will die happy.'

The king shook his head. 'But that is so painful a death. How could I sever hands, feet, nose, ears, from a living frame? How could you die happy if you were to be cut in such a way?'

'Then, and only then, will I save my kin who live around me, O king. So many of my family have grown around me and in my shade. What pain, what devastation would I cause were I to fall entire upon them, tear them to the ground even as I fall.'

The king rose, his face earnest. 'And this is why you wish that we cut you piecemeal, O forest lord? That you would save your kindred, and yet, you will die…'

'And happily would I die if my kin are spared.'

King Brahmadatta bowed low. 'So noble-minded a god art thou, O lucky tree. You seek to save the dwellings of your fellows even as your own is destroyed. Nay, we will bid our craftsmen seek elsewhere…' He beat his forehead…'but why? That we build to stand out among the kings of this land! This is but vanity. Have no more fear, for there shall you stand even if all else disappears.

And the Jataka says that king Brahmadatta gave generous gifts and alms at the root of the great sal tree and good fortune attended him and his people all his days. Today, the elaborate ceremonies that attended the felling of the 'auspicious post' or *magul kappa* is not observed. No longer is wood needed for columns except in certain architectural designs, but as we know, great trees always provided the columns of old. In times long past, the *mi* tree[30] was always chosen in the building of *sangarama*[31] for devales, *sinhasana*[32] and *rajamandira*.[33]

Duttha Gamani was puzzled at the reports.

'It is that the tree devata wishes to speak with thee, great one. And she wishes that we prepare no other abode for her. It is as if she would relinquish her home to thee only.'

'And is this what her words promised?'

'It is hard to know her intent, lord. But she awaits thee. That did she say.'

The morning was noisy as it always was in the city. Duttha Gamani, robed in simple white and accompanied by his umbrella bearer and ministers, walked to the parkland where, beside the ancient pillar of prophecy, stood the na tree of the devata.

'Who is it that sits there?' the king asked.

The chief minister peered from under a hand held over his eyes. 'A monk, lord, brown-robed—or is it that the yellow has browned with age...he sits beneath the tree.'

On their approach, the monk turned his head, looked at them with grave eyes. He was frail, old, and the dust of a long journey stained his bare feet. His face was age-lined and coppered, and his robe, certainly brown, rested upon him with the same heaviness of age. When Duttha Gamani had made obeisance, he spoke in a thin, rusty voice. 'I am of the place where the ancient Raddematamal pirivena once stood, O king, and where now is the hermitage of the great na forest. There rise the rocks that are as the colour of young roses. It was in the time of anguish that I retired to that recluse from the Kolombahalaka vihara near Raheraka.'

Carl Muller

'We have not heard of such a pirivena, holy sir.'

'Few have indeed, for there, beside the village of Ulpothagama, is the solitude where arahats have walked for thousands of years. It is only the forest now, but there, among the red rocks, lies the peace of centuries.'

'And what brings you here from the solitude of this na forest?'

'I have answered the call of the devata. To this tree has she now come, but her home is there, in the giant na of the forest, a tree she surrounds with the scent of her presence.'

'Know you then why she has come here?'

The monk shook his head. 'But this do I know. She left the na forest on the day you were ready to march upon the city, and here has she remained.' The thin shoulders raised slightly. 'She remains, perhaps, as a guardian, O king. Many moons ago did she give me her name and she said that you would wish to take her abode and that you would not be denied. And I thought—I thought you would come to the na forest, seek to fell the giant na of her habitation. How could I know that this na tree was her new abode?'

'Her name. How do we call upon her?'

'Swarnamali, sire. That was the name she gave me. But here does she call herself Ratnavalli, and it is by that name that the people worship her. And two gemstones too did she give to me...'

A thin musical tinkling filled the air and Duttha Gamani gasped as looking up, saw the tiny figure that stood agleam in the crook of a branch, threading the dark with a luminous blue. 'The Kota Liya,'[34] he exclaimed. 'It is you, is it not? The spirit of the stream?'

His mind raced back to his retreat from the ford, how the devas had urged his flight into the kills of Kotmalaya, even as his father sent a mighty force to slay him. And there, by the rushing stream that he named Kota Liya Ella, beside a line of humped rock had he seen her—a woman so tiny that she was no more than four hands high.[35]

'We meet again, disobedient one,' the devata tinkled, 'and now I have much to tell thee. What think you I am? A spirit of the waters, a forest elf, a tree goddess? Compose yourself, Duttha Gamani, greatest of kings, noblest of sons, doughtiest of men, for I have much to say. Let us not stand around even in my shadow. See, the grass is sweet and the dew has long dried.'

Duttha Gamani sat himself down, cross-legged, before the old monk, and his ministers in a crude half-circle. The woman stood, seemingly suspended between the branches, her hair streaming like polished ebony, her eyes of sunfire.

'You plan to build a royal residence—a dagaba, in the place where we first met, do you not? There, where the great river system furrows the foothills. It is well, for that is a place of great promise. Much do I know, for I have been ever with you, followed your steps, watched over you as you took the road of war out of Magama up to the gates of this city. Hold out your hand—your palm…'

The king's fingers closed upon the stone that materialized on his palm. 'My amethyst!' he exclaimed. 'Was this also sent by you?'

'Aye. To you and your brother. So rashly did you set upon each other. Think you how the course of your life would have changed had you killed your brother. Think you that you would have won your way into this kingdom with the blood of your brother upon your hands?'

Duttha Gamani lowered his head. The amethyst warmed his hand and again, his thoughts sped back to that terrible day when his men faced his brother's forces. He had led his army to Dighavapi, determined to defeat his brother, take back his war elephant, bring his mother back to Magama. And there, between his horse's ears, at the crest of the mane was this amethyst.[36] Even as he struggled with his thoughts, he felt the emptiness of his hand. The gem had disappeared.

'Attend on my words, noble one, for first must I tell you that this tree is yours to fell. This is but my station where I have remained to watch thee, stay close to thee. Here, in this lovely plain, will rise the greatest dagaba the world will ever know, now, and in the ages that reach to the edge of eternity will it stand, and always the name remembered. My home is everywhere, and I will remain in the high rocks, the trees, in the ponds of the lotus and in the rivers, aye, even in the rills that bring the water into the city. But even as you fell this noble tree and set your artificers, craftsmen and builders to work, do as I instruct. Let he who fells this tree be of moderate hue, neither too dark of complexion nor too fair. No blemish must he have on his body, no, not even if it were as small as a gingelly seed. He must not be a man too short of stature or too tall, and he must be young so that there be down upon his cheeks and chin, yet matured enough that he have hair upon his chest. Also, must the hair of his head fall free like the train of a peacock, unbound and unknotted. I see that your wise men take note. That is good, for such a man, and such a man only shall bring down this tree.'

'It shall be as you say, and good spirit, we thank you—the kingdom and we. Is it that you are called Ratnavalli as our people say you are, or Swarnamali as this good monk believes you to be?'

'Let it be as the people of this kingdom honour me. I am Ratnavalli, and in the solitude of the great na forest, which is my retreat in times of peace, there am I Swarnamali. But heed me now, for I must tell you of this land and of this place upon which your greatest work will you carry out. Think you that this very spot upon which grows this tree was but a wasteland and a wilderness? The noble Vijaya did come here, and so was the throne of the lion established, but this was also a great centre of trade and the meeting place of civilizations even 250 centuries ago. There, in the north of the great continent was Ujjeyini[37] and then there was no dividing sea and people came here from many regions. This city was the centre of trade of the south and here was the doctrine of of the great Sakyamuni[38] embraced in ages too distant to think of. I tell you this, for even as you prepare to dig, to lay the bases of the great thupa, do so with care. Surely will your builders come upon the relics of those distant days. Excavate the segment of the south with caution. There will you find the glazed alms bowls that belonged to followers of the Buddha many centuries before the coming of the arahat Mahinda to the Missaka mountain.'[39]

Duttha Gamani listened, entranced. Who would have thought that this city, this land he now ruled, had seen a flowering a thousand times over and been known and hailed in ages past, had risen to pinnacles of glory many times over. Who were these ancients the spirit spoke of, and how old was she? 'Is it that you have witnessed all this and seen the rise and fall of such people?' he asked.

'Age means nothing and nor does form. But know you, Duttha Gamani, that the greatness that sits upon and within you is of a quality that none can excel. Never has it been so in the past and never such in the years to be. This is why I have watched, showed myself to you even as you marched out of your father's kingdom, dejected of spirit. Many are the visions that men hold before them, but yours surpasses them all. And here, in the greatest of cities whose origins are shrouded in the mists of unknowable ages, will you cause to rise the greatest Buddhist city of all. This will it be—the principal city of this lovely land for many centuries, and to this place will the most treasured relics of the Master be enshrined. Its greatness will lie in its Buddhist heritage and from here will the doctrine go beyond these shores.'

'And will we endure? Will the passion of new remain the passion of the future?'

'It will, for the passion will throb as long as the doctrine continues to enlighten this and other worlds. But the glory will be dimmed as by a dark glass and times of travail will muffle the lion's roar. This, in the ebb and flow of time, will come upon the land and there will be a rending of spirit. Ah, but that is yet a time and time away.'

Duttha Gamani bowed his head. 'Then can we but do all we must,' he said.

'That you will. What matter if the ages of tribulation bury it? Burial is but the way of the earth to embalm the glory of man's endeavours. Will not in a later age, man unwrap the past to gaze in wonder at what has been achieved?'

Truer words had never been spoken. Even today, the greater part of Anuradhapura lies buried, but so far, patient and loving hands have unwound the bandages of the earth, drawn aside the coverlets of centuries to marvel at the structure and artistic planning of the city. Weerasinghe[40] asks us to imagine a garden city with elegant buildings glistening in the tropical sunshine, set in a mosaic of trim green rice fields with irrigation canals and tanks as far as the eye could see, reflecting the sunlight from their clear surfaces like so many mirrors and silver streamers in a setting of green. He enthuses at the great white dagabas with their gilded pinnacles rising heavenwards, as though indicating the ways to Nirvana.

The royal party returned to the palace and with them the monk of the na forest who wished to perform his ablutions and make salutations at the Maha Vihara. He was certain that Ratnavalli would return to the forest hermitage where the na trees grew in such profusion.

'Let it be known that none shall enter that holy place,' Duttha Gamani said. 'No woodsman shall ply his axe there and no collector of firewood shall pluck a twig from any tree that grows therein. Let it remain a refuge of the ascetic and they who seek to meditate.'

Yes, the great na trees tower there to this day and the faithful walk slow-footed along its ochre paths. They bow to the devas of the trees, sit upon the roseate rocks, gaze towards the holy mountain of Mihintale and lose themselves in a trance of faith and peace.

Carl Muller

Duttha Gamani summoned the chief of his guard. 'Find the man who will fell the great na. The wise ones will tell you of what man he should be.'

Now would the work begin.

Towering Faith

THE *MAHAVAMSA* TELLS US:

> The lord of the land had the place for the thupa dug out
> to a depth of seven cubits to make it firm in every way.
> Round stones that he commanded his soldiers to bring
> hither did he cause to be broken with hammers, and then
> did he, having knowledge of the right and wrong ways,
> command that the crushed stone—to make the ground
> firmer—be stamped down by great elephants whose feet
> were bound with leather.

As we now need to say, this book, preceded by its first
volume, *Children of the Lion*, follows, as closely as this
narrative permits, the *Mahavamsa*—the Greater Chronicle
as it is called. The writer wishes to state at this point that
many could and would question the thread of, and the
recounting of such narratives. The word 'vamsa'—and the
history of the Vamsa literature in India is fairly old—is
taken to mean *tanti* or lineage, and carried with it the idea
of lineal succession. Thus do we have the *Buddhavamsa*
which offers the history of twenty-four Buddhas and which
carries a later supplement that deals with the Buddha-to-
be. Geiger[41] thought the *Dipavamsa* represented the first
unaided struggle to create an epic out of already existing
material. This is the oldest-known Pali chronicle produced

in Lanka: the literary production of a school or community and not the composition of an individual.

Malalasekera[42] considers the *Dipavamsa* to be the last of the literary works of Lanka which had no special authors. Yet, this may not be altogether correct for the opening lines of the Vamsa entreat people to 'listen to me'—a form of supplication made by a narrator or an author.

As this story unfolds, it must be understood that while this work is based on the *Mahavamsa*, it will be necessary to note the disparities between this and other Vamsas and narratives. In his *Ceylon Lectures*, B.M. Barua noted that the *Dipavamsa* remained silent on the rise of later Buddhist sects in Lanka, and calls attention to the disparities, especially to the rivalry between the monks of the Mahavihara and the Abhayagiri.

It is fortunate that the writer has resolved to present this work as a novel, fleshing out the history of this island. It keeps readers clear of the major religious controversies of those times. Sadly, however, this cannot be altogether avoided, for the kings, as we know, were immersed in the religious ethic, and we find, as we progress, that it was necessary for the rulers to sometimes 'cleanse' the Sangha, even take sides in sectarian presumptions and squabbles. Suffice will it to consider what the *Dipavamsa* had to say about such issues:

> The Bhikkus of the Great Council settled a doctrine contrary—altering the original redaction, they made another redaction.
>
> They transposed Suttas[43] which belonged to one place to another; they destroyed the meaning and faith in the Vinaya[44] and in the Five Collections.[45] Those Bhikkus who understood neither what had been taught in long expositions, nor without exposition, neither the natural meaning nor the recondite meaning, settled a false

meaning in connection with spurious speeches of Buddha; these Bhikkus destroyed a great deal of meaning under the colour of the letter. Rejecting single passages of the Suttas and of the profound Vinaya, they composed other Suttas and another Vinaya which had the appearance of being genuine...[46]

It is hoped that the reader will understand the many pitfalls that loom before the writer. Whatever can be made of the wealth of chronicle, it is felt that one has to agree with the author of the *Mahavamsa* when he pointed out that the main drawbacks of the earlier chronicles were that in some places, they were too diffusive, in some too concise, and that they abounded with repetitions.

It is also hard to accept as entire even the story of the *Mahavamsa* without the *Atthakatha Mahavamsa*, whose literary position depends on Pali versions in the Commentaries. As Law[47] decidedly says, the *Mahavamsa* stands as a masterpiece in the Vamsa literature of Ceylon, produced by the poetically gifted thera Mahanama. Malalasekera[48] may have begged to differ, stating that Mahanama was no genius and that the author-priest was too hidebound by tradition, but again, Geiger, upon whose translation of the *Mahavamsa* the writer is much indebted, has observed that the chronicle has every claim to be regarded as a work of art, and in it one sees the hand of a poet.

What we must impress, as the story unfolds, is that the chronicles of Lanka have as their kernels, history and nothing but history. And who would not, in these narratives, accept both religious and patriotic motives, the belief in miracles, the wonder workings of the gods, the supernatural, the inventive power of imagination, the legends as well as the sober historical truths?

Carl Muller

An edifice of towering faith—this was what was awaited, and the city teemed with activity. Engineers became, at the outset, the men with whom Duttha Gamani held the most earnest consultations, for the king was made to understand that what he would now do was to also create for all time, a 'cloud fence' that the land required. As he listened to his engineers, he realized that the wisdom of the arahats was far too comprehensive to be cabined within the limits of doctrine only.

'But this is of tremendous significance,' he exclaimed. 'You say that this great thupa we build will be a bringer of rain, a boon to the people of this land?'

'It is for this reason, lord, that the site of this dagaba has been so ordained and such wisdom lies in the selection.' They placed before him the long line they had drawn—a gently curving line running through the crude near-triangular figure. 'Let this be the land, sire, and there in the north is the great dagaba of Nagadipa. Thus does the line descend and here, in the bulge, is the dagaba of Mahiyangana where first didst thou battle the Damilas. And see, lord, how the line falls to the southern sea where the great dagabas of the south lie. A line across the land, and as we see it, such a line makes of the land two like parts to east and west. And see where this line travels, lord. When the Maha Thupa is raised, it lies on the line too.'

'This is extraordinary, what you say. Is it that the ancient prophecies make out that such thupas, those to the north and south should lie on a line such as this?'

'Wise indeed were the ancients. We have thought on this for long and sought to understand how the clouds soar over us and how they sometimes give us rain and sometimes not. The rains come from both east and west, but oft-times they fall upon the coasts and often do the clouds scurry past and the rains do not come upon us, because, lord, from the point of the dagaba in the north to the point of the dagaba at Mahiyangana, the line is weak. Now, with the rising of the Maha Thupa will the line strengthen and no longer will the clouds pass us and deny us the rain we seek.'

Duttha Gamani turned to his mother. 'We find this puzzling. This line we speak of: It is here upon this parchment, but what line do we see that is drawn across the land?'

Vihara Maha Devi seemed to have other things on her mind. She gave a little frown. 'Our engineers are the mainstay of the land for it is their knowledge that has made the realm so well watered. How could we sustain so many, grow so much, if it were not for their efforts? This is a line they see, and if it be in their minds, they speak true. Who else can give such shape to the land as they do? And this is the line, drawn here, that they tell of—from the dagaba of Nagadipa to the dagaba of Mahiyangana, and then to the dagabas of the south. And where the thupas rise do the clouds come, as they say and bring their precious water. But here the clouds have passed us by. Were it not for the great lakes and ponds, what place would this be?'

'We agree, and is it that the weakness of this line will be no more after the rising of the Maha Thupa?'

'That is what they say. Who knows, but they are not given to careless presuppositions. As engineers do they see the clouds, not as we do.'

Even today we have come to recognize the genius of those engineers of old. Truly did they not wish a cloud to pass by, withholding its promise. It has been seen, studied, and now known that the line of large dagabas lying across the land are, in truth, an electrostatic fence. The largest dagabas seem to have been deliberately stationed on this line, from north to south-east, passing close to the central hills—a line that is now known to lie across a well-chosen ridge.

M.L.J.R Fernando[49] has shown that the shape of the dagaba and the cloud over it is similar to the 'point action' in electrostatics. He refers to a negative charge in the earth's surface and its vertical field intensity which is about 120 volts per metre. As such, the bulk of trees induce rain by charging and discharging electrical activity. Likewise, dagabas are rain inducers since static electricity is the key to unlock the water carried by clouds.

Fernando had even advocated that this could be proved by building four dagaba-like metal structures at the four corners of a 1,000-metre-sided square, pointing each structure at 30 degrees to the vertical, inclined towards the centre. If, with cloud activity, the whole is electrically activated, the neutralization which occurs between the cloud and the structure will bring down rain. He had recommended a network of such cloud control stations running both parallel and perpendicular to the great dagaba line which will cover the whole island, all computer-linked and with photoelectric cells that can discern the parallel rays of light from the sun, moon and stars, that will help to detect clouds.

It has always been a riddle and an enigma as to how the ancients acquired such knowledge. The very glory of Anuradhapura, the fact that this city of the lion was the envy of south India, that it was the most prosperous kingdom of the region, could only be because of the marvellous techniques of irrigation, of water storage and regulation, of a true scientific application that made the city the greatest then known.

Even the late Sir Arthur C. Clarke, seer of the Space Age, had looked upon the 'unexplained mysteries' of Sri Lanka's ancient grandeur and acknowledged the advanced scientific techniques and disciplines applied by the ancients.

Duttha Gamani expressed his thanks to the engineers. More than ever had he reason to fulfil the prophecy. The great thupa would bring added prosperity to this parched land. It would bring rain!

The silver was brought in from the refineries, the roseate bricks, the gold and gems carried to the vaults. Even as the excavation was being made, pavilions of *gokkola* were quickly constructed within which the king would remain to watch how the work progressed. These temporary pavilions were artfully built out of the pliable yet strong leaves of palm fronds, cut just after they emerged from the pod of a new branch. Gokkola is easily woven and its fashioning is both artful and complex.[50]

It was also necessary that the best butter clay be used.[51] 'Only the finest, venerable sirs,' Duttha Gamani told the monks of the Maha Vihara.

'Then must we bring such clay from where the heavenly Ganga falls upon the earth,' said the chief monk.

'Does the sacred water of the river also course the sky?'

'That it does, O king, for this, the river of the gods,

flows through the atmosphere and then does it fall to earth where the far mountains are. And some water yet stays in the air to descend unseen between the waters of the Varna and Asi. It is there that we can obtain the clay we need. Also, from the surface over which the river flows, it descends into the earth and continues its career to the regions of the underworld.'

'But how do we obtain such clay. Will it not necessitate a long journey and much time?'

'That it will, but even as in the building of the Lohaprasada were not the plans of such a palace brought to us by those monks who had overcome the *asavas*?[52]

'Will these saintly ones also go to the sacred river, to the place where this clay is?'

'They will. There, where the water is copper-coloured under a coppered sky. It will not be as far away as they have travelled before and their meditations in that place will cause the clay to rise and return to this place, for from one holy place can such be brought to another holiest of places.'

Duttha Gamini thought of the songs of the sacred river. How often had he heard them, even as a boy. The waiting women in his father's palace would sing and croon and the words would melt in the air:

Woodlands heavy with wild jasmine,
Embrace you with their fragrance,
Nearing your approach
Young plantain trees
Burst into sudden blossom...

How truly did the people hold fast to the old times, even those times before their times. He had listened to the invocation to the sacred waters of the great continent at the times of ceremonial bathing:

Om Gange ca Yamune carva Godavari, Sarasvati,
Narmade, Sindhu,[53] Kaveri jale'smin sannidhim kuru...

Hail O ye Ganges, Yamuna, Godavari, Sarasvati
Narmada, Indus and Kaveri, come approach,
Hallow and purify this water... [54]

His mind slipped back to the day when, but a stripling of
thirteen, he had stood beside his father at the sanctification
of the Badagaldora vihara.[55] Yes, much water was purified,
charged with spiritual power, at that ceremony.

'But the holy ones must go to Varanasi[56] of the Kasi
kingdom.'

'Where the devas will welcome them, O king. How much
do we hold that holy city to our hearts. There it was, at
Isipatana, that the Enlightened One preached first to the
monks of Pancavaggiya. Four sacred cities do we hold dear
in Jambudvipa: Kapilavatthu, Buddhagaya, and Kusinara
are the others. And do not the Jatakas always testify to the
glory of Varanasi? Two rivers[57] gave it its name, O king,
and it stood together with Campa, Rajagaha, Savatthi,
Saketa and Kosamba—the six great cities in the times of
the Master.'

'And would you not go as well, holy sir? We see that
even the thought of this city stirs thee.'

The chief priest looked up and then to the place where
the elephants were tethered. 'The Kasappa Buddha[58] was
born there,' he murmured, 'and in the Nikayas[59] and other
texts[60] are his discourses to be read. Know you, lord king,
that in the times to come, when the Buddha-to-be[61] comes
into this world, it will be Baranasi that will be the great
capital of all Jambudvipa. It will be a glory of 84,000 towns
and no more will it be called Baranasi but Ketumati; and
there will reside the Chakravattin[62] of the name Sankha

and this great king will renounce the world and become an arahat under the merciful Buddha.'[63]

Duttha Gamani nodded. 'Truly is there much the sacred texts tell us of. And will you prepare the monks that they may bring in the sacred clay?'

'It will be done.'

Acala, the assistant to the master builder came up and bowed low. 'The stones have been well trodden in, sire. Is it that we bring in the bricks that they be in readiness once the clay is spread?'

'Do so. We will wait upon the will of the devas for the spreading of the clay.'

'Lord king, many layers will be needed to reach the surface. Twelve layers is the estimate given.'

'Know you Acala—hmm, wait—are you not called Bhaddaka?'

'That too is my name, sire.'

'Well, know you that the *ayatana*[64] is also of twelve layers?'

'Forgive my ignorance, lord, for I am but a builder.'

Duttha Gamani smiled. 'And excellent in your work. The master builder speaks well of you. Let the bricks be readied. Say to the overseers that twelve layers will be as the starting point of awareness. Thus will the thupa rise as a living thing and be immortal.'[65]

When Acala had bowed himself away, Duttha Gamani ran a hand over his head, twelve bases! Of course—his grand thupa will be as a living thing!

It was indeed a day of days for the king. He had not sought to inquire why his mother had not come to the pavilion as he thought she would. She did not seem to show as much interest in this, his greatest work. But suddenly she was there. There was a gaily decorated archway at the gates, pennants of gold lining the path to the ornate doors. The guards were in ceremonial attire and the palace women wore festive dresses. She stood at the door of the hall and she was smiling. She raised her hands and her bangles of gold glowed.

'We have a prince,' she said, 'and the signs are being read and he awaits thee even as he sleeps.'

For a moment (and who would hold this against him?) Duttha Gamani forgot the work of the Maha Thupa, the clay he sought, the precious material he would use, the innumerable number of things that demanded his attention.

'A prince, our son. Fair of features and unblemished. You have a son!'

A son! He stared. He had hardly given thought to the affairs of the palace, to the women in their quarters beside his chamber, to the young girl he had made love to so madly. His heart quickened as he looked wide-eyed at his mother. 'Is, is the child ready to be seen?'

'Look on him to your heart's desire, our son, then can we listen to the wise ones.'

He held out a hand. 'You knew of the nearness of the time and all the while you told me nothing. We felt you were preoccupied with other things and were concerned. What of the mother?'

'She is well and does not ask of your absence. She is such a treasure and quick to understand and accept all that you need to do.'

'That is good. No queen can she be, but will receive much favour. Let her be decked with gems and have a chamber set apart for her…no, let her be moved to our chamber, so that all may know that she reigns over the women's quarters.'

'Then you? What will be your chamber?'

He laughed. 'Why, will not that be our chamber too?'

Vihara Maha Devi made a dove-like movement of her head. 'How little have you laughed. We have heard it so infrequently that we were sure you had forgotten that too. Come, we will look on your son.'

Tissa was overjoyed at the news of the commencement of work on the Maha Thupa. 'Say to our brother,' he told the rides he had summoned, 'that even as he embarks on this blessed enterprise, we have constructed and are also constructung, in faith and brotherly love, the dagabas we agreed upon. He will know what we speak of and he will be fired with the will to go on. Say that as he places stone upon stone, so do we, and that our labours are tied, one to another by the faith and love we share. Take him our greetings and to our mother this letter. Say to her that her son, Saddha Tissa longs to wake to the day when she will be in Ruhuna again.'

Tissa looked on the large dagabas he had begun to build with a mixture of love and sadness. Yes, he had done much to erase the grim memories of the past, of the days when, in pride and hatred, he had gone to war against his brother. Even as the enmity had dissolved, even as Duttha Gamani had begun his onslaught on the Damilas, the arahats of the south had guided Tissa, given him much to do. Hadn't Duttha Gamani bade him remain king of the Ruhuna realm, grow the rice that was so important, ensure that the south remain rich and self-sufficient? Internecine war did no good for the land when ploughshares became swords and one brother's hand was raised against the other's.

Following the advice of the monks, Tissa rebuilt the vast Dighavapi reservoir and prepared the rice fields so long abandoned. Even when Duttha Gamani came back and received the adulation of the people, he had been proud to show how green the land was, how the waters of the Dighavapi smiled at the sky and how work was progressing on yet another lake, the Ethimale tank.

Duttha Gamani was worried. Was not Tissa pushing himself to extremes? He thought of the wagonloads of rice sent across the river to feed his conquering army. Yes, Tissa had been unceasing in his labours. He had inspected the site of the new tank, considered the immensity of the undertaking and had clasped his brother's shoulders. '*Athi malli*,'[66] he had said. 'Surely this is enough? Do not drive yourself in this way.' Athi malli! Is it any wonder that both the reservoir and the village around it were called Ethimale—and this is its name to this day.

Duttha Gamini had made no comment. 'If that be your wish,' he said eventually, 'it is our wish too. Let it be known, by such a work, that love lies even beneath the thickest layers of hate.'

'Ah, but we never hated thee,' Tissa said simply

'That we know. Nor did we hate thee. Had we borne such hatred we would have sought thy life as you lay hidden in the Dematamal vihara. Yes, brother, build the dagaba. Surely will it mean something to those who will rule this land after us.'

Tissa had worked feverishly, and the Chulangna dagaba[67] was raised in atonement.

Duttha Gamani received the messengers with much joy, for they would take back to Tissa the news of the birth of his son. He had already ordered a week of rejoicing, and drummers and criers had fanned out, telling of the glad news.

'Let our brother cease his work for this short time and come to us, that we may share this joy. Say to him that we have not yet started to build, so let him, too, cease his work. He wishes to build another stupa at the site of our second encounter. That is as he wishes and we see why he desires to do so—the first to commemorate his victory, the second ours. It reminds us that we are not infallible, not invincible and none can understand victory without the taste of defeat. Aye, let him build. Say to him that it must be the largest in circumference in the south, encompassing the field of our battle. But also say to him that we await him, for our joy will be heightened when he is here. Also, our mother will be so pleased. He asks that she come to Ruhuna. Gladly will she if he would be here to accompany her.'

The chronicles do not tell whether Tissa came to Anuradhapura to look upon the infant prince, share the revels of the palace, look upon the land where he would some day be king, but it is easy to think that on so important an occasion, he did.

We also see, to this day, close to the Chulangana, the imposing Yudaganawa dagaba, considered the largest in circumference in the south—985 feet. It was on this ground that the amazing battle between horse and elephant took place and where Duttha Gamani bested his brother. Yet, as we now know, Tissa never did complete this work. Years and years of labour took its toll on both brothers, one building the greatest dagaba in the north-central kingdom; the other matching stone for stone in the south. Years of labour...while the little prince grew and became a handsome youth. Later, we are told by one school of historians that another king, Maha Parakrama Bahu, completed the Yudaganawa dagaba. There did he cremate his mother, queen Ratnavali, and renamed the dagaba Ratnavali Cetiya. This may be accurate or not, but it was seen how in Anuradhapura and Ruhuna, the faith rose, towering, touching the sky.

It was easy to convey the rock. Around the fastness of the Arittha mountain, that is also known as Ritigala, was gneiss rock in plenty, straight-veined and easily chiselled into convenient slabs. Duttha Gamani went to the mountain where, in the years before him and at the tail end of his own campaign, so much blood had been spilled. This was where the redoubtable Panduk Abhaya, when king of Lanka, had built his palace fortress as he plunged into battle with his seven uncles.[68] In this place too had Duttha Gamani destroyed the last of the Damila resistance and had not stayed to take in all that the mountain offered. But he had learnt of Panduk Abhaya and saw with pride the ruins of the old palace, the lichen-scarred and bleached pillars, the colonnaded passageways and stone balustrades. Again, he thought of the genius of the engineers, the builders. Why, there was a water drainage system that still worked, and even fountains.

But it was not the ponds or the rising walls of the fortress that the Damilas had occupied, that held his attention. It was the tunnel—so airy, spacious, so well cut...a broad underpass, a comfortable subterranean passage. It lay

Carl Muller

behind the pond, and he ordered the entanglement of vines removed.

'This did our ancestor cut over 200 years ago. Can a cart travel within?'

'Sire, it is large. Two elephants could walk within, side by side.'

'Let all the rock we need be drawn through it to the city. Carts can carry the lesser metal and elephants draw the larger stones. We will not obstruct the roads and cause hindrance to the people.' In this way, using the old tunnel that led to the city, thousands of tons of rock were moved, the activity scarcely noted by the city dwellers.

'We must prepare the mountain for the bhikkus once more. The Damila general who seized this place has desecrated it.'[69]

How marvellous it was to receive the chief priest the next morning, who said, 'The butter clay that surrounds the sacred river thirty yoganas round has been brought, O king. This have they who journeyed hence returned to say.'

Duttha Gamani rose excitedly. 'Brought here? But who could carry such a quantity. A mountain of clay would it be.' He strode to the balcony, looked out. 'No mountain do I see.'

The monk nodded wisely. 'It is surely there, sire. Now must we repair to the Ambalatthikka[70] where the saintly elder will lead the bhanakas[71] of the Suttas of praise.'

'Pardon our lack of faith, holy sir, but it is that we must go down, see for ourselves.'

'Do so, O king, and know how kindly the gods look upon thy work. Will there be a large pavilion raised in readiness for the dighbanakas wherein white cloths must be spread?'

'That will be done.'

'It is well. The Venerable Dhammapada Abhanaka Mahatissa will surely lead the devotions.'[72]

Duttha Gamani went to the site to find the builders standing around, their faces full of wonderment. 'Lord,' said one, 'at what time was this clay spread over the crushed stones. It has been done so well and so evenly that we cannot think how such work was done at night.'

Yes, there was the butter clay, kneaded lovingly between the stones, spread in layers of ash-milk, smooth as a porcelain saucer. 'Sire,' said another who hurried up. 'There, beside the far wall and running beside for a great distance is a river of clay such as this. Thick as many pythons does it lie and no finer have we seen. Its moisture makes it like alabaster.'

Duttha Gamini was too full to speak. The gods of the holy river had made of the work a miracle. He called a courier. 'Go ye to the Maha Vihara and await...no, go to the Ambalathikka where the chief priest will be and say that we wish, until the time of the completion of the thupa, that the Sangha accept alms from us. Hurry!' He then told the builders, 'Now will we lay the bricks and upon them a rough cement that will receive the layers of *kuruvinda*.'[73]

Hundreds swung into action, and as he watched, the linen was being spread in the largest of the pavilions and pots of water placed beside the entrances. The dighabanakas came in single file, talipot fans in their hands and, with the chief priest, a number of monks. Duttha Gamani made obeisance.

'Your message have we received,' said the chief priest gravely, 'but we do not consent to the receiving of alms. Rather, let the work go on.'

Carl Muller

'But how else can we honour the celestial ones? We beseech you, allow us to show our gratitude.'

'It is of no necessity. This work will take many years. Much more is there to occupy thee.'

'A year, then? A year of alms. Is not that but a token?'

'No.'

'Half a year?'

'No, O king. Truly does your heart overflow, but not even half a year.'

In vain did the king plead. Three months...one month... then he said, 'One week. One week is poor recompense indeed. Who knows, we may need to ask more of thee. One week?'

'Very well. One week.'

Duttha Gamani was pleased. Bowing low, he called to his craftsmen. 'Eighteen large pavilions must you construct around the site that a great alms-giving may we conduct.' He made way for the dighabanakas, called for a drummer and flautist to usher them to the place prepared.

'They will recite the *Brahmajala Sutta*,' the chief priest said.

'And this will be in thanksgiving for the great boon given us, holy one?'

'No, but it will recall to us the wise teachings of the Master...and even as all employ themselves in this great task, their devotions will fill the air and fix for all time the sanctity of this place...for this will always be a sacred place. Indeed will this city and all its pillars and arches, roads and dwellings be known as holy.'

The sonorous chanting began and with it a great peace seemed to steal over the morning.[74]

Even as Duttha Gamani listened, the arahat Indragupta came to him. This was the sainted monk who guided the court and discoursed to the royal family. It was necessary, he said, that once the layer of ruby was laid and secured with a mesh of iron, the whole must be sprinkled with sweet-scented marumba.

'Marumba, holy one?'

'Sire, it is the sweet-scented extract of the Himalayan herb that bursts into glorious flower. The perfume must be sprinkled, for the butter clay must hold down the iron upon the cinnabar and over this must the marumba be copiously spread. Worry not, for I will instruct the monks to cause the scent to be brought hither.

Duttha Gamani nodded. He had little need to question how such would be done, for the marvels he had seen and the power of the saintly monks over time and space could not be denied. 'Great vials of such scent will we need,' he said simply.

Arahat Indragupta moved away. The sprinkling was necessary even as the clay melded over the cement that held the iron. Let the heavenly ones do as they think fit.

Again did the astral forms float out, this time to the ranges of eternal snow where, in the long crevices of snake-grey, did the marumba grow. There also did the devas gather, and in the sun-dazzle of the heights, celestial maidens sang their devotional songs.

'Carry with thee yet another thought,' the chief priest had told the monks. 'Ask of the holy ones that the relics of Ramagrama[75] which are now in the possession of the Naga kings of the world below, be sent here, for how else will the relic chamber be filled?'

How easy it is to say and to know with certainty that faith built this huge dagaba. What could be really achieved without faith? Duttha Gamani had ceased to wonder, to question. He knew that all the art and craft of the kingdom lay at his disposal, but what could all this achieve without faith?

The foundation with its twelve layers was completed. Every layer over what had been already spread by unseen hands was worked in with the butter clay. Duttha Gamani prostrated himself in silent thanksgiving when the city awoke to the sweetest pall of scent that enveloped it. Over the ground, a soft mist arose and every leaf of every tree was dipped in dew. A gentle rain, so fine that it was as a precipitation of smoke-water, seemed to blanket the pit of the foundation. His nose twitched as the fragrance curled over the palace and in it was the lingering attar of balsam and rose, a confection of jasmine and magnolia, the wafting scent that ascetics believe come only when the *siddhas*[76] danced.

'Surely is this the scent of the marumba,' Duttha Gamani said, as he held his palms to his face. 'It showers upon the clay and its perfume waves softly over us all.' He rose, hurried out. Everywhere the people of the palace stood entranced, heads lifted, drinking in the heavenly odour. Even the peafowls in the courtyard were strutting around, exclaiming at the falling powder-like dew that spattered its brilliance on the grass.

He was not surprised to see a group of monks of the Maha Vihara approach. The arahat Indragupta raised a hand in benediction. 'Make offerings of the five kinds of lotus,'[77] he said, 'for more benevolent have the gods never been.'

'Tell me, venerable one, could there ever be such a tree or flower that gives such delight to the senses. This marumba, which is of the Himalayas…surely it is a plant of the celestial world.'

Indragupta's voice was grave. 'Of that none can be certain, but many are the flower trees of the celestial regions. I had thought, perhaps mistakenly, that it is also what we know as Mandara, which is also a celestial tree, but that tree, whose wood gives a fragrance stronger and more lasting than sandal, is hard to find in this land or the lands around the Himalayas. And that, we are told, is a tree; not a plant that yields flower scent.'

With the ceremony of the lotus offerings, the sun began to sponge away the dew-drip and slowly, almost stealthily, the heavenly perfume stole away, withdrew from the city until it gathered upon the huge basin of clay. The chief priest was pleased. 'Now must a substance of worth be placed upon the clay, and the pure crystal stones of the mountains are fitting indeed.'

Again, we would wonder at this suggestion, for a layer of crystal, we imagine, would be purely to embellish. Since these layers would be covered, any idea of embellishment would have been empty indeed, but there had to be reason why crystal needed to be one of the twelve bases.

In Sri Lanka, the moonstone, also called sandakenmina, is said to be a variety of crystal. It is also called diyathirippu because it is believed that when the beams of the moon fall on it, the crystal becomes exceedingly moist until drops of water trickle from it. The gem districts of the island abound with crystals and we are told that Duttha

Gamani used 'mountain crystal'. Indeed, crystal was used in the construction of the so-called 'moon chambers' or balconies, where the reflection of the moon caused them to glow and cast back the light.

We learn in the *Hansa Sandesa*[78] of the beautiful city of Jayawardhanapura thus:

> The crystal wall girdling this city
> Shines like a deep and mighty billow
> Dashed against the extremity of the shore
> When Vishnu, king of the gods
> Was stirring the milky ocean with Mount Meru...
> The radiant moon reflected from
> The crystalline balconies, seemed as if
> The moon enraged at being outshone
> By the beaming faces of this city's damsels,
> Had left its wonted course through the heavens
> And had descended with galaxies of stars
> As in troops to wage war with these damsels.

Mountain crystal, as was laid, was quartz, and quartz as we know, has the property to store, amplify, transform, focus and transfer energy. Also, it has the ability to hold an electrical charge.

Again we ask: What immense knowledge of so advanced a nature did the ancients possess? In this age, this year, even as these words are written in the twenty-first century, we know that a tiny slice of crystal, a silicon chip, can store large amounts of information in the form of energy in the microcircuitry of a computer. As an amplifier, crystal can take an electronic charge and increase the flow of energy, which is why quartz is used in amplifiers, microphones and loudspeakers. Our photovoltaic cells show us how crystals transform solar energy into electricity. They are also used in lasers for focusing energy. Where would our modern-day electronics industry be without the crystal?

It has now been outlined that crystals vibrate energy at all of the colour frequencies and this vibration is very similar to the vibratory pattern of the human body, having a dramatic effect on the human energy system. Myers[79] called this stored energy of the crystal 'Piezoelectricity'—in other words, crystal in a receptacle, a storage bank that provides some of the earth's energy.

Earlier in this chapter, when discussing the great dagaba line or 'cloud fence' that runs through Lanka, it was not mentioned that the *kotha*—the top of the pinnacle of each dagaba, was of polished mountain crystal. Was the kotha then made to function as the final rain-inducing trigger? Who can say...but suffice it be recorded that over the marumba-soaked clay was a layer of mountain crystal placed and upon this were stones spread, held in place by the butter clay. Then, using the strong resin of the *kapittha* tree[80] mixed with the sweet water of the golden coconut [81] a sheet of copper of a thickness of eight inches was laid. Leaving this for a month to set, arsenic was then dissolved in sesamun oil and liberally applied over the copper which would be the 'glue' upon which was pressed a sheet of silver, seven inches thick.

The time had passed on fleet feet and it was now the middle of the year and the month of Asatha was upon them. The arahat Indragupta had taken leave of the palace, wishing to depart to Jambudvipa. He would convey to the faithful the news of the rising of the Maha Thupa, and would return with many to do it honour.

Now was it necessary to allow the huge foundation to rest. It was also time to assemble the craftsmen and artists

Carl Muller

and hold much discussion. Duttha Gamani was weary. He found himself tired at rising, tired at retiring. The years had taken much of his fire, his spirit, and he walked with a slow step. He had a long wait now, and he found much joy with his son who was growing to be straight and tall and with great good looks. The astrologers had read the signs of the child's birth and he considered them idly. Why, he had hardly had time for the little prince.

He clapped his hands, told an attendant, 'Say to the prince Saliya that we wish him to come to us.'

Saliya

Vihara Maha Devi told her son, Tissa, that she would return with him to Ruhuna. 'It will be but a short visit, our son, for you see how much our presence here is needed. Your brother has much to be concerned with and the work on the Maha Thupa drives all else out of his mind. Now, happily enough, there is a long wait until the foundation settles and the wise ones say a sign will there be for the resuming of the work.'

Tissa went to the window. 'An enforced wait. Yes, that should give him the rest he has denied himself. How concerned was he at the work I had embarked on. Does no one express such concern here?'

Vihara Maha Devi sighed. 'He has always been of iron determination. Even on the day you arrived, did you not see how greatly the devas have favoured his efforts? Now, more than ever does his mind rove unceasingly. He has sat at the feet of the leading monks since the arahat Indragupta went to Jambudvipa. He has become enamoured of the will, the passion and the powers of the gods and he asks unceasingly of them. The pious monks tell him much, and he listens, but ten days ago he spent many hours with the thera Dhammagutta—or was it the thera Kuddhatissa—I'm not very sure...and also with the holy Teraputtabhaya who was one of his champions. He goes to hear the discourses of Mahatissa of Bhaggari and Mahanaga of Kallivallimandapa; spends the greater part of the mornings listening to the theras Mahavyaggha and Mahavimsaka. The bhikkunis Mahila and Samanta have been exhorted to teach the Vinya throughout the kingdom. Others too: the bhikkunis Girikali and Dasi; and now does the bhikkuni Kali, with a retinue of almost twenty thousand, fare across the land.'

'And you, mother, has this not been a joy to you?'

'Oh, it has, it has...yet—it...it has weighed upon me for much lies upon me...and...and there is the prince. Now does his father wish that the boy be his companion and son, and together they go where the father wishes to go.'

Saddha Tissa eyed his mother with some concern. 'Tell us,' he said softly, 'what is it?'

She looked at him uncertainly. 'What—what is what?'

'What is it?' he asked again. 'Is it that you are ill? We see many care lines upon a face that was once as soft as a pigeon's breast. How can a queen be as a king—for that is surely what you have set yourself to be.'

They looked at each other silently for long moments. It was Vihara Maha Devi who dropped her eyes first. When she spoke, the sound seemed to come from far away. 'You remember, our son, of the days of your boyhood...you and your brother: two disobedient ones to be sure. Ah, how you caused your father to worry and fret and sit for long staring at nothing, wrestling with himself. And even then, young were we and youth absorbs so much. Nothing jars the frame, takes its toll on mind and body as age...'

She began to sing softly:

At the wewa, egrets rest in trees
Their beaks are of gold, having no silver;
Having no muslin, they are bright in cambric,
At the wewa, egrets wade in water...

'Do you remember, our son?'

Saddha Tissa laughed. 'How can we forget? We would sing such songs even as we went to the ponds and lakes that fed our fields. Wait—there is another verse. Let us think...ah yes...at the wewa after bathing, the egrets perch on trees, having no clothes they wear white head cloths—having no silver, their beaks are of gold; at the wewa the egrets wade in water.'

'But you must sing it. How well did you sing it long ago, you and your brother, as you marched through the tall grass with your bows and arrows. Come, sing the other verse. We will sing with you.'

Gently, Tissa took his mother's hands. 'And will you sing as we journey back. There will be three strong carts piled with cushions. Horsemen will clear the road of every stone, and your waiting women to tend you throughout. Oh mother, what love awaits you in the land where you were truly queen.'

'Sing with me,' she said softly.

At the wewa, good lily clumps there are
To gather those, good women go,
Making black, making white, they cook the rice;
To eat the rice of the lily seeds there is no curry.

They were silent. Outside, the road beyond the walls erupted in little spirals of dust as a wayward wind raced helter-skelter. Tissa rose, shook his head. 'Tell us please, is there anything that ails thee?'

'Go now. Tell your brother that we return to Ruhuna but for a short time.' She raised her dark eyes and they mirrored the old fire of a youthful queen who had seen one son ride to glory, wade through blood to victory. Her eyes told of dreams come true. 'We are—we are so tired,' she breathed.

Thirty-six million bricks! It is seen how a country may have natural resources in abundance, but material advancement does not depend on the extent of wealth but upon the way it accrues and is employed. Even as the city of the lion became one of the greatest in the ancient world and remained the capital of Lanka for an astonishing thirteen centuries[82] it stood as striking evidence of the great natural resources of the land, just the way this was demonstrated in the ruins of the Yucatan, the remains of Nineveh and the pyramids of Egypt.

What are our reactions today to the massive labour that rose as a tide to meet the dreams and aspirations of the kings? It has been commented by Wall[83] that when a nation's resources are:

> expended in luxury, pageantry, wars and other forms of unproductive expenditure, these are lost to all beneficent purpose, and is productive at best, of a transient glory, destined either to perish in oblivion, or to endure as proof of the neglect or selfish ambition of irresponsible despotism.

However, he admitted that religious and educational institutions cannot be regarded as wasteful or unproductive:

> insofar as they tend to increase knowledge, instill virtue and extirpate vice, they are to the highest degree useful and profitable to the State by promoting order, peace and morality.

It is true that in those far-off days almost all countries were ruled by despots or patriarchs. As such, the fruit of all national industry could be consumed, wasted or converted to reproductive use according to the whims of the sovereign. Wall also noted that:

> One, animated by beneficent ideas, might devote the labour of the people, the resources of the country and the energy of his own character to the construction of an useful work; another, more vain and selfish, might neglect such work and, like Cheops, apply the national sinew to a stupendous pyramid, for no higher purpose than to calculate his horoscope or to perpetuate the memory of his personal vanity.

Perhaps there is a lesson to be learnt here. But it is hardly correct to surmise that the eventual fall of this great city led to an unhappy, desolate people who clung to the expiring remains of the great enterprise they represented.

However, the fact remains that the position, the power and the resources of kings were derived entirely from the industry of the people. It has been very often said that had the Sihala possessed the wisdom and foresight which led the Chinese to fortify their country against invasion, things would have been so very different. Wall[84] noted that if it weren't for invasions and harassing interruptions, Lanka would have enjoyed a continuous permanent and enduring wealth:

> The Sinhalese would almost certainly have attained a degree of intellectual and moral refinement and culture which are fairly foreshadowed by the art displayed in the design and decoration of their religious edifices; the science exhibited in the conception and execution of their stupendous irrigation works, and in the beautiful ideas of

Carl Muller

womanly devotion and female virtues which form a staple
subject of their best poetry.

He added that:

The Sinhalese attracted their rapacious neighbours to their
defenceless coasts by lavishing upon their religious edifices
a profusion of precious metals and gems which were highly
prized and easily carried off by their enemies.

Was this massive glorification of the faith a political
mistake and economic mistake? It is true that with the
arrival of Mahinda came the seeds of a cultural renaissance,
visible in the literature and the plastic arts, but what became
obvious to many was that the island and Anuradhapura were
no longer a hermit kingdom. Even Ptolemy's map of Lanka,
made eight centuries after the arrival of Vijaya, identified
'Anurogramam'—the city of Anuradhapura. Megasthenes
met Sihala envoys in the court of the emperor Asoka's
grandfather, Morya Chandragupta; and Ptolemy was told
by voluble seafarers that Lanka was reputed for honey,
ginger, gems, gold and silver, and the long luxurious hair
of both men and women.

And now…thirty-six million bricks! A giant stupa indeed.
Later we will learn of even greater edifices, but as the
bricks were assembled, as the labour went on, it was plain
that this would be a giant among thupas. That this marvel
could have known decline is in itself utterly astonishing, but,
as Wall[85] said, Lanka's Damila neighbours were rapacious
and they came to plunder, finding invasion easy. How true
it is that strong fences make good neighbours. Alas, the
people of Lanka never built strong fences.

Even as prince Saliya rode out with his father, the boy did not really seem to enjoy himself. Duttha Gamani found his son withdrawn, introverted and altogether too effeminate. He blamed himself for neglecting his son and yet, he felt slightly uncomfortable. Why was the boy so, so unresponsive?

They were on a hard road that made every hoof beat a drum crack: the road that dipped between fields of rice and lost itself behind lines of boulders, rain trees and twisted fences. They were to visit the beautiful rock monastery of the Issarama, a pastoral shrine known as the Isurumuniya today, which had been lovingly constructed by King Devanampiya Tissa in the third century BC.

Duttha Gamani had raised an eyebrow when he had asked where he wished to ride to.

'The Issarama,' he had said softly.

'But you often go there. Do you not wish to visit the camp of the champions? Have you learnt to wrestle and draw a strong bow? You are fast becoming a man and you are not as muscled as you should be.'

The boy dropped his eyes, said nothing.

'Very well, to the Issarama then. It is a pleasant ride and we like the country around it.'

Saliya mounted his pony with ease. His lithe girlish figure sat well and the reins lay lightly in his hands, the polished leather snaking around his lean fingers.

'Do your teachers overburden you?'

'No, father.'

'And do you not spend too much time among the women? You mother encourages this, we fear. What is it among the women that you find of such interest and amusement?'

'They teach me art, father. I learn much of design and colour and of the ways of embellishment, and how gemstones are used in design and the composition of substances.'

Duttha Gamani knotted his brows. 'But that is the art and accomplishment of women, our son. Is it that such appeals to you? You have many companions, have you not?'

'Yes.'

'Many?'

'A, a few, father. We play and swim and shoot our arrows in the park.'

'A few, eh? And who are these companions? The sons of noblemen, we warrant.'

'There is Maheja and Diyavasa, father.'

The king tensed. He had heard strange stories that the women of the harem tittered over. 'Maheja is no fit companion for a prince, our son. It is said that he spends too much time in the guards' quarters and has brought shame upon the head of his father.'

Saliya flushed. 'But—but he is a good friend. No wrong has he done me.'

'Humph! And what do you say is right and what is wrong?'

The boy did not speak. What could he say? Could he tell his father of the many hours he had spent with Maheja in the little room behind the deserted shrine of Pura Deva?[86] It was such a quiet cobwebby place where they had stood so often, embraced and told each other of their love. Such a beautiful body had Maheja. His dark eyes were curtained with long lashes and his flesh was as a luscious berry. Saliya had been shy at first, shy to even say how much he adored this older boy, and then there was no more to think about as they slowly unfastened each other's clothes and their embrace was fierce and demanding. Yes, Maheja could do no wrong. Maheja loved him, gave him those first exquisite sensations of sexual joy. They would sit on the cold stones, fondle each other and throb with their ejaculations.

'You are as beautiful as any girl,' Maheja would say, and Saliya would crimson and snuggle closer, his body craving a love he could not understand.

It was Maheja who told him of the evenings he would spend with some of the royal guards in their curtained quarters, while the moon rose outside. They were rough sometimes, he said, but they would take him with speed and hold him fiercely while the hair of their chests and beards inflamed his body and tickled the back of his neck. He had wished to perform in the same way, and Saliya, unmindful of the discomfort, made no objection. All he knew was that he had to hold fast to this love. The devas knew he had so little of it.

'You see what lies ahead, our son,' Duttha Gamani said. 'We are now truly a people. We have united all of the people, wherever they be, under one banner. Thus have we prepared a future for all of our line, and this future is yours.'

Saliya understood what his father was trying to tell him—that now was the rising of Sihala nationalism: a nationalism that was coursing through the healthy young blood of the country; the rising of a new race under the order of Buddhism. Surely, he thought, all the people of the lion were Buddhists now.

'But father,' he said, 'this future you tell of. It is full of a new pride. Religious pride as well. Is such pride necessary?'

'It is. How else would we have rid ourselves of the Damila rule? You are young. All this will be manifest to you in later years. It is the doctrine of the Buddha that binds our people together.'

Saliya made no reply. He wondered instead what his father would say if he knew that his son was, what? A dreamer...a lover of beauty...a strange inward being who found love in the arms of men and spent long hours reveling in his nakedness in the privacy of his chamber. He was so amused at the merit book his father kept.[87] How devotedly did the *lekhaka*[88] enter all that his father accomplished: the building of cetiyas, the alms given to the Sangha, the good deeds... He leaned forward in the saddle. He could see the bulging rocks of the Issarama and, along the line of rocks that skirted the footpath beside the pool, the mouth of the cave where he had sat, listened to the tales of the carver of the elephant and held his breath as the man had begun to stroke his thigh, then eased his rearing penis from the inner wraps beneath his tunic. The man had been well pleased at the prince's fervent response.

'One day must you lie with a woman,' he had chuckled, 'and I will watch and make a tablet of stone that all may see and know how well I have schooled you.'

The carver was a straight-limbed man with eyes of grey fire and hands that always seemed to be moulding an imagined form. Saliya had responded to him with a quickening he found impossible to control. 'I will come as often as I can,' he breathed. 'Do you—do you love me?'

The carver had smiled. 'Love you? Do you not know how beautiful your body is? Softer than any woman's. Your eyes sing, and your mouth is rich. Rubies paint your lips and your neck is slender. Oh, love you I do, for you are the woman that lies in the heart of every man. Say to no one what we do here.'

'That will I never do.'

Even as they dismounted, Saliya's eyes sped along the line of rocks. Surely the carver's chamber had been an old dwelling of ascetics. He felt pleased when his father stopped to admire the carver's art. On both sides of the rock, on the eastern side, where a fissure led to a shining pool, the man had begun to shape the forms of elephants that would soon play among the lotuses in the pool.[89]

Duttha Gamani watered his horse, bade his son do the same. The breeze rustled the leaves of the spreading bo tree whose roots drank deeply of the water. He watched his son, who was on one knee, picking off the burrs on his pony's feet. So graceful—and so like a girl. He even fluttered his eyelashes, his hands, as a woman would. The astrologers had been cryptic when they read the signs at his birth, examined him for body marks.

'He bears the mark of the Padma Nidhi,' they had said, 'and thus will he be compassionate by nature—a lover of beauty and precious things, and be filled with strange thoughts of the ascetics and celestials. Such a treasure of Kuvera as he has been granted gives him the qualities of a goddess—a *svattwika*. It is a mark characteristic of a *nidhi* that is seated deep within the mind and is strongly feminine.[90]

'And what of his future? What do the signs say?' Duttha Gamani had asked.

'His wrists are pale-coloured. He will have much happiness. An even belly does the child have. He will seek pleasure and know various pleasures. There is some fear, lord. For see how blue are the lines of his palm. Such tell of unchaste desires and there are rows of reddish hairs on the line of the shoulders. He will not be a king, sire, for he will wish to bring himself down, not aspire to kingship.

It is a sad thought, for see how tight-stretched is the flesh upon his knees. A happy person will he be, loving, gentle, woman-like in his ways and yet will he seek to degrade himself and seek his happiness with the degraded.'

'And can this not be changed?'

'Let him be brought up as a true prince. Let him know all, learn all. Fill his days with manly ways, manly pursuits. See how plump is the head of his genital organ. That, too, is the mark of one who pursues happiness. Likewise are his buttocks plump and fleshy and the wrinkle of the navel is not straight. Let him not be encouraged to seek the company of unworthy women.'

Duttha Gamani had dismissed the astrologers, turned to his mother. 'Unworthy women indeed. Who such is there? What do these old men mumble about?'

Vihara Maha Devi had smiled. 'A son so beautiful. Let not what they say trouble thee. He will be our prince and as worthy of you as you were of us.' She dimpled. 'What manly ways can we teach to one who can now only turn to the breasts of a woman. That time is yet to come.'

Duttha Gamani had stared, then laughed. 'Truly, our mother, are you wiser than all.'

As he watched his son standing beside the soft green of the water, watching the ripples widening from the muzzling mouths of the horses, he felt that he was very far away from this young straight-limbed boy whose heart danced to a music he knew not of. What would be his life? Surely he would be king...and yet, could he be as a king? Duttha Gamani had little doubt that Saliya would devote himself to the beauty of the city, for such a sense of artistry did he possess. Truly would he make the kingdom resplendent, but such a head would remain in rosy clouds and that would be a weakness that did not behove a king.

He sighed and walked to the little monastery and the shrine on the rock.

It must be of concern to many scholars that the story of Saliya or Sali is omitted from the ancient manuscripts. In particular, we refer to the *Sahassavatthu Atthakatha*[91] of unknown authorship. The *Mahavamsa Tika*[92] has three references to the *Sahassavatthu Atthakatha* concerning stories of Suranimala, Gotayimbara and prince Saliya respectively, but while the first two, the champions of Duttha Gamani, are to be found, the story of prince Saliya has been altogether omitted. It is left to us to ask why the story of the prince was ignored by whoever copied the original manuscript. Was it that it was considered unsuitable, or that it would diminish, in some way, the glory of the father?

Saliya knew that his father would spend time listening to the old thera who was supervising the building of a stairway and platform. A young samanera, dark-skinned and round-faced, was sweeping the path beside the pool. 'The kumaraya has come again,' he said in a bird-like voice. 'See, on that tree the guavas are full-grown and ripe.'

Saliya smiled. 'And you cannot climb. Cannot you be a boy any longer?'

The samanera laughed. 'That I am, but robed, as you see, it will not be easy. Also, I may not.'

Saliya placed a foot in the crotch of the tree. The guavas hung heavy, pale green and full-bellied. On a high branch, a squirrel made a meal of one, scattering little bits of the white pulp. 'I will pick some for you. Will you take them to the refectory?'

'Yes, and I will say the prince picked them for me.'

Carl Muller

With ease, Saliya swung up the tree, picked the largest of the bunches, tossed them to the boy below. The squirrel ting-tinged indignantly but refused to leave its meal. It sat, making little jerks of its crouching body, its tail bristling.

'Will you eat one with me?' Saliya asked.

The samanera shook his head. 'I thank thee, but the *loku sadhu,* our chief priest will not like it. I will take them to the meal room.'

'Well, this guava is mine. I give it to you. Eat.'

The boy grinned. 'The prince commands it?'

'We do.'

'Then I must say I cannot eat alone.'

'How so?'

'It is not befitting.'

They laughed merrily. The samanera propped the broom against a tree. 'These are fine guavas.' They squatted and ate their fill.

'Now will I pluck you more to take to the temple,' Saliya said.

'Do you go to the old cave at the end of the road? The carver has gone. He said he would go to Rattala[93] to visit friends.'

'But he will return?'

The boy nodded. 'The loku sadhu wishes a *makara*[94] of elephant heads over the stairway.'

In the tiny hall, Duttha Gamani was in earnest conversation with the old monk who insisted that the Issarama be a place of relaxation and not over-grand like all the other sacred edifices that lay around it. 'I encourage the artists to depict the joys of life, sire. A holy place to be sure, but one where the faithful understand the simple pleasures that are so strengthening in their pursuit of the good way. Look on the way the birds compose themselves…

and how the trees burst into flower. Truly is all nature such a happy thing. And are we not one with it? Or must we be ever burdened with the many man-made austerities that make of us but strangers to the celestial and natural order?'

'But—but we thought that the decorative art that is here is…is…'

The monk gave him a quizzical look. 'Is frivolous, O king? And is not this human existence also a frivolous thing that, with the snap of a finger, can end?'

Duttha Gamani received the monk's blessing, wondering at his own existence. Had he ever had time to be frivolous, to relax, to enjoy himself. Was he living his life or simply propelling his soul before him? He saw Saliya approach.

'So sweet it is, father. We kept this guava for you.'

'Hmmm. And have you made offering of such to the temple?'

'The samanera took many away, but this one did I keep for you, and some I ate.'

They rode back as the sun began to burn down on the fields and insects droned high-pitched in the hedges. Even as they approached the city, Saliya drew on the reins. The sound of singing came to him, soft, honey-sweet. He had heard it before.

Duttha Gamani turned in the saddle. 'Why do you stop?'

'It is nothing.'

They rode to the inner courtyard. The stablemen hurried up to lead the mounts away.

'Through the season of rain and two dry seasons must we allow the base to remain, sire,' said the master builder,

Carl Muller

'for each of the sections must knit and be bonded with the other.'

'So long!' said Duttha Gamani.

'That it is, lord, but think of what pressure the base must withstand. The rains must come that we may see how well the ground sits. This is what the engineers also say. Then the dry weather must hold the surface clay fast. A long, hot spell must follow, and if there is rain, yet another dry period is necessary.'

'But that is over a twelve-month, is it not?'

'Yes, sire.'

In 1979, Lankan scholar, R.A.L.H. Gunawardana, spoke on 'Ethnoscience and Technology in Pre-colonial Sri Lanka' on the occasion of this country's Archives Week. He declared that:

> The historical understanding of the technological aspects of our pre-colonial civilization can by no means be called adequate.

James Emerson Tennent[95] has given us short descriptions of manufactures, metalworking, engineering and science in ancient Lanka, but it is now known that many of these British writers wrote with a strong colonial prejudice.

Yet, as we know, scientific thought existed and to a very great degree at that; and the ancient Sihala were well versed in irrigation engineering, metallurgy, civil engineering, hydraulics, the construction of immense monuments and even with such disciplines as anatomy, physiology, pharmacology and phytochemistry.

Is it any wonder, then, that the ancient Chinese spoke of the excellence of Lanka's craftsmen and artists? Famous

Chinese writers made much mention of this, among them being Kao-seng-chuan, Liang-shu and Kuang-hung-ming-chih.[96]

In the *Rajatarangini*[97] we are told of a variety of fine cloth called *wdihan sinhal*[98] that was imported from Lanka.[99] Also, Pliny[100] tells us of the Sihala ambassadors who came to the court of the emperor Claudius. They were so well versed in astronomy that they made observation of the night sky of Rome, told of how the positions of the stars differed when viewed from Lanka, and discussed the position of the star Canopus. As it was, a famous Roman astronomer had tried to determine the circumference of the Earth on the basis of the position of Canopus as seen from Alexandria and Rhodes.[101] It is no wonder that the *Suriyasiddhanta*[102] makes many references to Lanka in relation to astronomy.

We are also told in the *Gira Sandesa* (message poem of the parrot) of how students of the Vijayaba Pirivena[103] plotted the location of planets by using cowries on a blue board and moving them according to their calculations.

Irrigation engineering had developed to such high degree that giant tanks, more than 15 miles in circumference, were constructed. Certainly, knowledge of heavy construction existed and Duttha Gamani knew of the precautions taken by builders. The base of the Maha Thupa had to be firm enough, evenly distributed enough to take the weight of the thupa. Compaction had been well done and the brass and iron and silver that had been laid would form an immovable centre of the great circle of the dagaba... a mass of solid brickwork, rising 270 feet would need a foundation of an exceptionally substantial character.

'We will build that it will stand beyond time,' he exclaimed.

'We must then give it the time it needs, sire.'[104]

'Yes, we will be patient. But let the craftsmen and artisans assemble. Much do they need to prepare.' Rising, he gestured his acceptance as the builder bowed. Striding to the corridor, he saw, through the arches of stone, the prince talking with a group of palace ladies. The boy was examining a richly embroidered cloth, doubtless praising one of the women for her excellent needlework. He told a courtier to bid Saliya come to him.

'We like it not that you spend your time so. Womanly pursuits are not fitting of thee.'

The boy remained silent, a slight blush colouring his face.

'See how you redden! Go! Go and be a man!'

Saliya did not move. He felt his face aflame. Did his father doubt that he was a man? 'Father, do I not spend time with the women because I am a man?'

'And do you also drape yourself in the silks and shawls and headcloths and admire the tassels of their girdles? Is that also how you be a man?'

Saliya bowed his head. 'I ask your forgiveness, and yet, it is the beauty of the things I see that tugs me. Do I not perform as well as the noblemen—riding, fencing, wrestling, splitting the stave at archery, vaulting, and do I not run fleetly? Am I not as the others? The champions also speak highly of my prowess.'

'Yes, yes, all this are we told of, but do you do so because you enjoy being a man? Why think you so much of the accomplishments of the women? What pictures do you carry in your mind?'

'Pictures of great beauty. Petal colours, the sky with its lamps lit, the plains that smoke with the dust of horses. Is it not right that a man know such as these?'

Duttha Gamani sighed, sat the boy beside him. 'When we were as old as you now are, we were consumed with hatred and the passion of the warrior. We had a kingdom to conquer and battles to fight and armies to lead. A troubled youth it surely was, and all we could hear was the ring of steel and the clash of arms. We were the disobedient one. Duttha. Our father wished our death. Our brother too. But know you why we find pain at the thought that you look with such admiration upon a woman's garments...we did our father much hurt, for in our anger and pride did we send him a woman's garments and bade him wear them. We raised in him a terrible wrath and a terrible shame.'[105]

Saliya gripped his father's forearm. 'Have we not heard of all you did, and think you that I have not gloried in your greatness? In the city many poems are written and the people sing of your deeds. Every footfall of your great march out of Ruhuna is told of, again and again. But father, in this time of peace that you have given to all the land, is it still the time to think of warlike pursuits. Now, in the calmness of the land, can we not think of the things that are beautiful? Man will I be, but who can be a man such as you?'

Duttha Gamani felt his cheek twitch and wondered why. He covered his son's hand with his. 'We do not mean to be insensitive, our son. The queen will leave for Ruhuna with your uncle. Would you like to go too? It will be a short visit.'

'I think not, for I will surely be in the way. And father, did you not call for the craftsmen? Allow me to look upon their plans and designs, select the best.'

'That is good. Your artist's eye will be of use.'

'And you are not angered?'

'No, our son. We all find happiness in our own way. Go now, and be happy. The message has gone out to the crafts villages. They will be here in the morning.'

Saliya met Subha in the outer chamber, Subha, the son of the chamberlain. 'Oh my, have you spent much time with the king today. We can go to the walls, watch the citizens as we often do.'

Saliya hesitated, then said, 'There, beyond the outer walls, about a thousand paces to the south where the houses are screened by large rain trees...what is that quarter?'

Subha wrinkled his forehead. 'Thousand paces... but to the south are the hovels of the sweepers. Those of low caste. Why do you ask?

'You are certain of this? And do you pass that way?'

'Rarely.'

'But it is on the road to the Issarama. I went there yesterday with my father.'

'So what is it to you?'

'Nothing. Those are chandala homes...are you sure? Subha nodded.

'Oh well...we will go to the walls.'

'In the corner of the wall where none may see us...'

'No,' said Saliya sharply. 'It is not right that we must fondle each other the way we do. I do not wish it.'

Subha shrugged. 'I thought it made you happy. It pleased you, did it not?'

Saliya made no reply. They walked on in silence.

Duttha Gamani had wished his son be recognized as *Adipada*.[106] Vihara Maha Devi thought it was too premature. 'He is yet but a boy,' she had said. To give him such title would be to give him a quarter to govern and his own company of archers.'

'Yes, for soon he must be ready. It is necessary that he be given a careful education and be aware of the responsibilities he must bear.'

'And who will be his guide? Did you not say to your brother that he will also be king of all Lanka?'

Duttha Gamani leaned back, drummed his fingers on the arm of his seat. 'Yes, there is that too. But will not Tissa be happy to rule over Ruhuna? He has sired many sons and the sweep of his domain reaches Kalyani[107] as well as the eastern shore.'

'Perhaps he will. But we feel that the prince is not ready. He does not enforce himself. We had thought that he be given a regal office at first.'

'Regal office? As a leader of the guard? Or a *sabhapati*?'[108]

'Yes, that would be a beginning. As a sabhapati he would proclaim the royal order, would he not? Also, he will be over the *Lekamge*[109] and there will be opportunity to give orders that redress grievances and have opportunity to move with the people too. Or better yet, appoint him the *nagara guttika*.'[110]

'That pleases us. You are wise as always mother. Such will give him true princely duties to perform, and the four quarters will he administer and officers of the units will report to him. And when do we declare him *Yuvaraja*—our heir?'

'Time will tell, our son.'

Duttha Gamani watched the entourage leave. The whole city was agog, thousands lining the decorated streets to watch the departure of their queen. Tissa took fond leave of his brother, promising that their mother would return in as splendid a manner as this, her leaving. The carts

Carl Muller

laden with gifts, were so many that Tissa stared. 'All this? By the gods! Will you heap on us the wherewithal for a year or more?'

'You must give of the contents largesse to the people of Ruhuna and to the brotherhood in our name. Also, must you offer alms at the holy places along the way, and brother, see that the rice growers of Dighavapi are well rewarded.'

It was a splendid affair for surely did Vihara Maha Devi leave as a queen of all Lanka. Drummers strode ahead, hours before, clearing the road, calling on the people to gather by the wayside. For days, the decorations had been raised and in every village along the route men and women had raised the arches, woven beautiful structures of gokkola and lined the route with flags of gold and red. Even the wayside trees were festooned and every holy place readied to bless the queen as she fared south. Platforms of areca trunks and matting were raised on which village girls would sing their songs of victory, and flower maidens, their baskets bursting, would scatter jasmines and fragrant Millingtonia[111] as their queen went by.

Vihara Maha Devi gazed fondly and not without pride as Saliya, gold-sashed and with a red-and-gold pennant on his spear, rode at the head of the troop of cavalry that would escort the party as far as Mahagamendi on the south road, from where a fresh escort would lead them west, the south again, then east. It was a comfortable road, easy on the oxen with their silver neck bells and gilded horns. Tissa rode in state, insignia bearers ahead, accompanied by his umbrella bearer and flanked by the chiefs of his guard. He would be met by his own dignitaries even as they moved towards the slopes of the hills that would take them to Ruhuna. But six days previous had riders been dispatched bidding that all ceremonies be laid on to receive the queen of the south, now queen of all Lanka. Tissa's own son, Lanja Tissa, would lead the four cohorts[112] and his mother would know once again how glorious the south was.

Saliya rode back, head high. He had taken duties as a *senapathi*[113] with a sudden awareness that this was what his father had wished—that he be a man. A surge of emotion flooded him and, at the outer walls, he swung his horse's head, shouted: 'Proceed ye to the citadel and disperse. Let it be known that we ride yonder. Also, do you give orders that the roads be cleared and the sweepers assembled early.'

Spurring his horse, he rode to where the trees rose high and unkempt hedges hid the homes of the low-caste scavengers. They too had watched, hidden behind their fences of thatch, behind high bushes, as the royal procession went by. They too had lit lamps of palm fronds and raised flags and tied flurries of cloth upon the trees. He eased his mount to a walk. Yes, this is where he had heard the singing, the sweetest he had ever heard, young, angelic, each note as pure as the earliest dewdrop. Who could sing like that in this lowly place? He wondered at himself…a prince, sitting uncertain in the saddle, looking upon a chandala quarter.

Riding past, he struck east, circling the place of the street sweepers. Ill-kempt plots, wild grass and bramble. The soil was a litter of broken stones and sharp white pebbles, but beyond, the grass was richer and margosa trees sprang from rumples of olive. Even as he passed a small rise, he looked around. Why, he was but a short distance away from the eastern wall, there where the *Hopalu*[114] grew in profusion.

Carl Muller

And then he saw her. He checked, stared, dismounted and held the muzzle of his horse. With care, he walked towards the girl, keeping away from the open spaces, knowing that there was little cover that would allow him to approach unseen. The girl was bent over, picking the fresh-fallen red flowers that lay like fleshy rubies on the grass. Reaching a sturdy tamarind, Saliya watched her. She had not noticed him. She filled a little basket with the flowers, then pinning one in her hair, sat beneath a tree, drawing and smoothing her cloth over her bare knees. With a little shake of her head, she began to sing.

The Chandala Maid

So sweet was the village of Mundavaka
Adjoining the banks of the swollen river,
The village where the homes were spread
With scented clay, and the floors all smoothed over.
So sweet the village of Mundaka
Where lived the craftsman Tissa,
Noble of bearing, full of peace and inner joy...

Saliya was entranced. The girl sang with a soft rapture
that made the very air sigh. This was surely her, the
songstress of the chandala quarter. And what was this she
sang of? The wise men who taught him so much, had once
told him of this village. He was certain he had heard of
it before. Mundaka! A tiny settlement, he had been told,
beside the great river far to the east and coursing from
the hills.

So noble the craftsman Tissa,
Filled with devotion, loving the doctrine,
Caring for the beloved Sumana,
His helpmeet, his woman, a gentle dame
In whom the blood of craftsmen flowed.
Full were they of love for the faith,
Full were they of love for each other...

The sun coursed westward and imperceptibly, the shadows grew longer. The girl rose, took up her basket, began to walk towards the tamarind. Saliya inched back, behind the trunk, stood still. She walked past, humming gently to herself. She had been so close. He stood, trance-like, unmoving. Only his eyes moved yearningly, as he watched her walk away. So, so beautiful. Never had he seen one so ethereally beautiful. Her walk inflamed him, yet he felt no rising carnal desire. He wanted to run, fall before her, worship her. Her hair, parted in three, cascaded down her back like rivers of jet. Her arms, her shoulders, her neck seemed enamelled, rose-touched, soft brown of the young berry, silken and sun-kissed. She carried her basket at her hip, and her short cloth, ill-cut at the hem, covered her but scantily. Knees dimpled as she swayed by, her calves slender, her ankles bare of chains. So young, he thought wildly. Her breasts were so firm that the nipples, like olive seeds, were a dusky pink. She wore no jacket and her cloth was knotted below her navel, below the slim waist, clasping her hips with a kind of reverence. Her eyes were so luminous—candid pools, the lashes long, fringing the twin ponds like rows of delicate sedge grass. Her lips, full and glistening, pouted slightly as she hummed, and her hips moved deliciously with every unhurried step.

Saliya held back, watched her walk beyond the margosa. She would surely see his horse, he thought, but she turned abruptly, made for the rear compound of the chandala quarter. Trembling slightly, he went to his horse, led it away slowly, then mounted. When he reached the palace, he was filled with an agitation he couldn't understand. He went in to change, take himself to the bath, while his attendant stood by with the cosmetics that would be needed.

A chandala maid! An untouchable! The daughter of one who scavenged, who cleaned the streets at dusk, who, if he had been told right, ate unclean meat. He paced his chamber restlessly. Was this true? Didn't his religious advisers say to him that no man was unclean; that within this Sihala structure of communal boundaries, there were no untouchables? Perhaps this was not as unsurmountable as it seemed. He knew of the old Brahmanical concept, but he also knew that although there was the organization of service castes, usually regarded as high-caste vassals, there was no real ostracism even of the chandalas. They were the lowest, surely, but they too had their role to play. Oh, he had to see this chandala maid again! He stared at his reflection in the grounded metal of a shield that hung upon the wall. He felt a pulse pounding in his head. He had to cry out, tell of what ate into him, made his knees tremble.

'I love her,' he cried. 'I love her! She will be mine!'

He flung himself upon the soft pile of his bed and wept.

Valentia[115] tells us that in the first decade of the nineteenth century, the Sinhalese were so mindful of their symbolic privileges that no man who wasn't entitled to such distinction could cover his house with tiles. If he ventured to do so, his house would be pulled down by order of his superior. Also, a poor tailor could be all but killed at the church door if he dared to marry dressed in a scarlet jacket. As Valentia said:

> The privilege of caste extends to the dress of females, and many are prohibited from wearing a petticoat below their knees or covering their breasts.

Carl Muller

Even today there is the general feeling that the low-caste person should dress with no ostentation and women of the Pali, Kinnara and Rodi castes[116] seldom wear a covering over the waist, avoid bangles, and the men wear no fancy sarongs, belts or shirts.

In Anuradhapura as would be expected, the farmers— the Goigama caste—were the most numerous. As late as 1899, Ievers[117] noted that villages were usually comprised of single castes, living in physical separation from others. He estimated that two-thirds of the Sinhalese villages in the North Central Province were Goigama, while there were other villagers of certain low-grade members of this caste. Ievers noted only nine mixed villages, and in his tabulation, gave us the following:

> Goigama (farmers) including the Vanni, a northern people who farmed the region; and Vellala, accounted for 618 villages. Next came the Moors with 108 villages; the tom-tom beaters, 69; the dhobies, 65; the blacksmiths, 53; and the Panna, 30; the Veddahs, 25; the potters, 16; and the Waggai, a lower grade of Vellala, 12.

There is no more absorbing study on all phases of Sinhalese social structure than the account given the world by Knox.[118] He distinguished carefully between the caste order and the feudal status of each, and as Ryan[119] tells us, Knox was quoted extensively by Daniel Defoe in *Captain Singleton* and it is probable that *Robinson Crusoe* also owed something to Knox.

The writer takes the liberty of quoting extensively from Knox's comments on caste, since it is felt that a greater understanding of the Sinhalese social structure will help readers understand the immense predicament Prince Saliya was rushing into:

Among the People there are diverse and sundry Casts in degrees of Quality, which is not according to their Riches or Places of Honour the King promotes them to, but according to their Descent and Blood. And whatsoever this Honour is, be it higher or lower, it remains Hereditary from Generation to Generation. They abhor to eat or drink, or intermarry with any of Inferior Quality to themselves. The signs of higher or meaner ranks are wearing of Doublets, or going bare-backed without them: the length of their Cloth before their knees, their sitting on Stools, or on Blocks or mats spread on the Ground and in their Caps.

They are especially careful in their Marriages, not to match with any inferior Cast, but always each within their own rank: Riches cannot prevail with them in the least to marry with those by whom they must eclipse and stain the Honour of their Family: on whom they set an higher price than on their lives. And if any of the Females should be so deluded, as to commit folly with one beneath her self, if ever she should appear to the sight of her Friends, they would certainly kill her, there being no other way to wipe off the dishonour she hath done by the Family but by her own Blood.

Yet for the Men it is something different; it is not accounted any shame or fault for the Man of the highest sort to lay with a woman far inferior to himself, nay, to the very lowest degree, provided he neither eats or drinks with her, nor takes her home to his House, as a Wife. But if he should, which I never know done, he is punished by the Magistrate, either by Fine or Imprisonment, or both, and also he is utterly ecluded from his Family, and accounted thenceforward of the same rank and quality, that the Woman is of, whom he hath taken. If the Woman be married already, with whom the Man of better rank lies, and the Husband come and catch together, how low soever the one be and high the other, he may kill him, and her too, if he please.

Carl Muller

And that by marrying constantly each rank within itself, the Descent and dignity thereof is preserved forever; and whether the Family be high or low it never alters. But to proceed to the particular ranks and degrees of the Men among them.

The highest, are the Noblemen, called Hondrews, and which I suppose comes from the word Honabrewne[120] a title given to the King signifying Majesty: these being honourable People. 'Tis out of this sort alone, that the King chooses the great Officers and whom he imploges in his Court, and appoints for Governors over his Country. Riches are not here valued, nor make any the more honourable. For many of the lower sorts do far exceed these Hondrews in Estates. But it is the Birth and Parentage that inobleth.

These are distinguished from others by their names, and the wearing of their cloth, which the Men wear down half their Legs, and the Women to their Heels, one end of which Cloth the Women fling over their Shoulders and with the very end carelessly cover their Breasts, whereas the other sort of Women must go naked from the waist upwards, and their Cloaths not hang down much below their Knees; except it be for cold, for then neither Women or Men may throw their Cloth over their Backs. But then they do excuse it to the Hondrews when they meet them saying, Excuse me, it is for warmth.

They are distinguished also by their own Countrey Caps, which are of the fashion of Mitres: there are two flaps tied up over the top of the Crown. If they be Hondrews, their Caps are all of one colour, either white or Blew; if of inferior quality; then the Cap and the flaps on each side be of different Colours, whereof the flaps are always Red.

Of these Hondrews there be two sorts, the one somewhat inferior to the other as touching Marriage; but not in other things. The greatest part of the Inhabitants of the land are of the degree of Hondrews...Among the Noblemen may be mentioned an Honour, that the King confers, like unto Knighthood, it ceaseth in the Person's death and it is not Hereditary. The King confers it by putting about their Heads a piece of Silk of Ribbond embroidered with Gold or Silver, and bestowing a Title among them. They are stiled Mudianna.[121] There are not above two or three of them now in the Realm living.

Next after the degree of Hondrews may be placed Goldsmiths, Blacksmiths, Carpenters and Painters. Who are all of one degree and quality. But the Hondrews will not eat with them: however in Apparel there is no difference and they are also privileged to sit in Stools, which none of the Inferior ranks of People hereafter mentioned may do. Heretofore they were accounted almost equal to the Inferior sort of Hondrews, and they would eat in their Artificers' Houses, but thereafter they were degraded upon this occasion. It chanced some Hondrews came into a Smith's Shop to have their Tools mended, when it came to be Dinner time, the Smith leaves work and goes in to his House to dine, leaving the Hondrews in his Shop; who had waited there a great while to have their work done. Now whether the Smith fearing lest their hunger might move them to be so impudent or desperate as to partake with him of his Dinner, clapt to his Door after him; which was taken so hainously by those hungry People in his Shop that immediately they all went and declared abroad what an affront the Smith had put on them. Whereupon it was decreed and confirmed, that for ever after all the People of that Rank should be deposed and deprived of the Honour of having the Hondrews to eat in their Houses. Which Decree has stood in force ever since.

Nevertheless these Smiths take much upon them, especially those who are the King's Smiths: that is such who live in the King's Towns and do his work. Those have this Privilege that each has a parcel of Towns people belonging to them, whom none but they have to work for. The ordinary work they do for them is mending their Tools, for which every Man pays to his Smith a certain rate of Corn in Harvest time according to ancient Custom.

But if any hath work extraordinary, as making new Tools and the like, besides the aforesaid Rate of Corn, he must pay him for it. In order to this, they come in an humble manner to the Smith with a Present, or a bottle of Rack[122] desiring him to appoint his time, when they shall come to have their work done.

Which when he hath appointed them, they come at the set time, and bring both Coals and Iron with them. The Smith sits very gravely upon his Stool, his Anvil before him, with his left hand towards the Forge, and a little Hammer in his right. They themselves who have come with their work must blow the Bellows, and when the Iron is to be beaten with the great Maul, he holds it, still sitting upon his Stool, and they must hammer it themselves, he only with his little Hammer knocking it sometimes into fashion. And if it be anything to be filed he makes them go themselves and grind it upon a Stone, that his labour of fileing may be the less; and when they have done it as well as they can, he goes over it again with his file and finisheth it. That which makes these Smiths thus stately is, because the Town's people are compelled to go to their Smith, and none else. And if they should, that Smith is liable to pay Damages that should do work for any in another Smith's Jurisdiction.

All that are of any Craft or Profession are accounted for an inferior degree, as Elephant-Catchers, and Keepers who are reckoned equal with the Smiths, &c. abovesaid, tho they neither eat nor marry together; lawful to but eat the jaggery they make (which is a kind of Sugar) but nothing else.

Another sort is the Poddah. These are of no Trade or Craft, but are Husbandmen and Soldiers, yet are inferior to all that have been named hitherto. For what reason neither I, nor I think, themselves can tell: only thus it falls on them by Succession from their Predecessors and so will ever remain.

After these are the Weavers, Who beside their Trade, which is Weaving Cloth, are Astrologers, and tell the People good Days and good Seasons; and at the Birth of a Child write for them an account of the day, time and Planet, it was born in and under. These accounts they keep with great Care all their Lifetime; by which they know their Age, and what success or evil shall befall them.

These People also beat Drums, and play on Pipes, and dance in the Temples of their Gods, and at their Sacrifices, they eat and carry away all such Victuals as are offered to their Idols. Both which to do and take, is accounted to belong to People of a very low degree and quality. These also will eat dead Cows.

Next to the Weavers are the Kiddeas or Basket-Makers. Who make Fans to fan Corn, and Baskets of Canes, and Lace Bedsteds and Stools.

Then follows the Kinnerahs. Whose Trade is to make fine Matts. These Men may not wear any thing on their Heads. The Women of none of these sorts ever do. Of these two last there are but a few.

All below the Couratto or Elephant-Men, may not sit in Stools, nor wear Doublets, except the Barbar, nor wear the Cloth low down their Legs. Neither may any of these ranks of People, either Man or Woman except the Potter and the Washer, wear the Cloth to cover their Bodies, unless they be sick or cold. Neither may they presume to be called by the Names that the Hondrews are called by; nor may they, where they are not known, change themselves by pretending or seeming to be higher than Nature hath made them; and I think they never do, but own themselves in the rank and quality wherein they were born, and demean themselves accordingly. All Outlandish People are esteemed above the inferior ranks. Names of the Hondrews always end in Oppow[123] and of others below the degree of the Elephant People in Adgah.[124]

The Slaves may make another rank. For whose maintenance, their masters allow them Land and Cattle.

　　　　　Carl Muller

While many of them do so improve, that except in Dignity, they are not far behind their Masters, only they are not permitted to have Slaves. Their Masters will not diminish or take away ought, that by their Diligence and Industry have they procured, but approve of it, as being Persons capable to repose trust in. And when they do buy or otherways get a new Slave, they presently provide him with a Wife, and so put him forward to keep House, and settle, that he may not think of running away. Slaves that are born of Hondrew Parents retain the Honour of their degree.

There is one sort of People more, and they are the Beggars: who for their Transgression…have by former Kings made so low and base, that they can be no lower or baser. And they must and do give such titles and respects to all other People as are due from other People to Kings and Princes.

Portuguese historian Ribeiro[125] also gives us this account:

Those which follow are the lowest castes: the tom-tom beaters go in war to beat their drums and they come back with their own company. The wood cutters live in separate villages which also belong to the king; they cut the trees which they are commanded to and they have to convey the stores and baggage of the army; and of this work they are so proud that in defeat they would lose their lives before their stores. There are workers in clay and the washers, the latter of whom wash the clothes, and the former supply pottery to all the village free of charge. The *Jagrieros*[126] make a kind of sugar from the liquor they draw from some trees, and of this they give a fixed quantity to the Lords of the village. The shoemakers, *Pachas*, and barbers are very low in caste, and they also have similar duties each according to his grade. The *Cornacas* are those who tame and look after the elephants; they live in separate villages the same as the *Pachas*, the villages of both of whom belong to the king; and it is the same with the villages in which live the

Chalias, the people who collect cinnamon; each of these has to render the number of *bahas*[127] at which his *paravenia*[128] is assessed, for all of them are not subject to the same amount of duty, some paying more and some less. They carry at their waists a small knife with which they strip the bark of the trees, as they enjoy the privilege of not being subject to any other kind of duty; they will not perform any service except what they are subject to, even if they are to be condemned to the fire, for they say that this would establish a precedent...

In her dung-floored hovel, the chandala maid squatted, laying firewood in the gap below the crude hearth and checking each stick. Some which seemed damp, were laid aside to be stored in the cradle that hung over the fireplace where the heat and smoke would soon make them dry. She rose, dusted her hands, turned to her basket of Asoka flowers which lay at the doorway. The flowers were as sweet mouths, and she picked up the basket with a little sigh.

Her mother, a firm-fleshed woman, high-breasted and with a ring of tissue around her ample hips, came in, tucking at the strands of her greying hair. Sweat stood upon the sides of her forehead, and she looked at her daughter with some concern. 'Flowers again...walking among the thorns in this heat. And what use are these flowers? Do we make a dish of them?'

'But they were fallen, mother. Who can pick them—they grow so high in the trees. See, don't they bring colour wherever they are placed?'

The mother smiled. She thought of the tiny settlement of Mundavaka where they had lived, where her daughter, Devi, was but a tiny big-eyed girl of three, where the great river sang in the days when the wind was balmy and kingfishers sulked in the grey branches of ancient trees. The Asoka trees would be in full flower there too, and she would carry her little daughter on her hip, point to the bright red heads of bloom, whisper stories of the forest, those cold magical places of the deep woods where leopards raised their voices of power and glided through the haunted tangles. And such a peace there was. The tiny village, the river, the wind-swept fields, the forest. Yet, Anuradhapura was the place to move to: a place of safety when the Damilas, cruel in their panic, killed and shredded, even as the prince of the south bore down, leading thousands to purge the land of their taint.

She sat, reached for her daughter's hand. 'Come, daughter, sit beside me. Know you not that you now cause us much worry?'

Devi sat, her hand against her mother's shoulder. 'Worry? But how do I worry you? Is it anything I do or do not do?'

'You are of that age...'

'Oh, so soon? Why, I am...'

'Hush. Look how the men around remark upon you. Ah, if only we were in Mundavaka. There did I know much peace. Here, in this city, too many look in too many places for the women they will take. How fortunate it is, indeed, that we are of the chandala ... and yet, your father is chief of the chandala and so it is that we must now find you a chandala partner.'

Devi tensed. 'No, not yet, dear mother. Why do you worry so? Is it that you find me a burden?'

'Child of my womb, what burden have you ever been? It is your father who worries too much for he hears the talk of others. Know you not that many have already sought to

be your partner? No, do not look so amazed. For over a
year now have you been so noticed and asked after.'

'But, but, a year? I was but a girl a year ago…'

'And more beautiful than any other, I say. And now that
the ripeness has come upon you, many seek you. Surely
you have noticed.'

Devi shook her head. 'I, I work, I sing, I gather wood…
and, and I'm not ready, mother. Why must you worry so?
Do you wish that I go away?'

They hugged each other. 'That will be hardest to bear,'
her mother whispered.

'Tell me of Mundavaka,' Devi said softly, 'of the story
of the birth of our prince. I can never tire of hearing it. I
have begun to make a song of it. Yes, truly a song, mother.
Tell me how our prince was born.'

It was a strange story whispered by some people, even
they of chandala village, also told of in the outlying river
villages. Devi had glowed, thrilled to it when she had
heard her mother tell of it many moons ago. She leaped
up, laughed, 'See, I will sing it to you…'

> So sweet was the village of Mundavaka
> Adjoining the banks of the swollen river,
> The village where the homes were spread
> With scented clay and the floors all smoothed over:
> So sweet the village of Mundavaka
> Where lived the craftsman Tissa
> Noble of bearing, full of peace and inner joy…

'My child, do not sing that others hear you.'

'To myself, mother. Only the wind listens, and the trees.
Oh mother, tell the story. More verses will I make and then
will I sing it when I am out in the fields and the flowers
will listen and the buds will surely open.'

'It was the jungle, my child, the jungle that crowded beyond the fields and the short rocks that were as the stumps of teeth. It was from that jungle that the Veddah brought to the craftsman a wild pig he had killed. Tissa and his wife Sumana had been kind to the Veddah, helped him with grain and strong bowstring and often had Tissa fashioned the iron points of his throwing stick and also shaped new bows for him.'

'They were good people, mother, loving and kind.'

'That they were, that they were. And when the Veddah brought to Tissa the flesh of the wild pig, Tissa was loth to receive it. Surely, he thought, could the Veddah eat well of it and put food in the belly of his woman and their sons. But the Veddah said no. "This food I give you is wages for the work you have gladly done for me. How else would I hunt and gather the honey of the wild bee if you had not armed me. This is in payment for but a little of what you have done." And Tissa could not refuse, and he called to his wife and asked her to cook the meat.'

Devi smiled. She loved to listen to her mother. 'And they made a grand meal of the flesh, I am sure.'

'Oh you funny girl. Know you the story and yet you test me with such remarks. Sumana made grand dishes of the flesh for sure. Some of it did she fry and some boil and part did she brush with honey and burn upon the coals and much did she cook with chillies and spices. And the aroma filled the house and Tissa fetched a large new pot into which the meat would go. But he would not eat despite the appetizing smell and the succulence of the gravy. "Cover the pot with a white cloth and let it be," he said, "for how can we eat until we make offering to a holy one?"'

Devi nodded. Now would Tissa cry out that a holy one, a saintly one hear him. Oh, she knew the story, but never tired of her mother repeating it.

'Tissa raised his hands, called out thus: "Without doubt, if true religious devotion be ours, will a saintly being come hither, receive this offering." And his wife whispered, "So much meat is there, O husband, cooked in five different dishes. Surely, one holy one will find it too much." And Tissa embraced his wife, praised her wisdom, and called out again: "In this fair land, fortunate beyond measure, if any holy ones hearken to my plea, let eight possessed of supernatural powers assemble here, come and receive these alms." He was filled with faith. He knew the holy ones would come, and he set to work preparing his house for their arrival. They gathered flowers to be floated in dishes of rose water and incensed the corners and lit the clay lamps that they burn through the night. In the clay pots, newly burnt upon an open hearth, did they place the golden flowers of the coconut and the brass lamp with the peacock design did they fill with oil and lay in each petalled dish the new wicks to be lit at nightfall. And it was late when they retired, the meat untouched in its new pot and the smell of it stealing outdoors as the night closed around them.'

'Oh mother, what a beautiful song will I make of this. Today do you tell it as you have never before. And the dream, mother, the dream...'

'Yes, my child. How well you know the tale. Perhaps you should tell it to me instead.'

Devi coloured. 'To one will I tell it...some day...'

'Oh, who? Your children?'

Devi ripened, blushed. 'No,' she said softly. 'Surely there will be one who would listen.' She lowered her eyes quickly. Dared she tell her mother of the tumult in her mind? Through the thatch fence she has seen the prince—Prince Saliya ride by. Surely was this his story…it belonged to him. One day, she dreamed, she would sing her song to him. 'What of the dream, mother?'

'It was in the small hours of the night when even the owl had stopped calling to the moon. Then did Tissa dream that eight beings entered his house, enveloped in astral light. They came through the walls and closed doors, even through the clay-slatted roof. He stirred, awoke and looked around. It was very dark, very still, but he roused Sumana. 'Our heart's desire will surely be fulfilled,' he cried. Then, as the first flush of the new day touched the trees beyond the river, he began to coat the floor with scented clay and raise a white canopy over the doorway. He went to his plot at one side of the house, selected and cut two fruit-laden banana trees which he carried to the threshold, making of them welcoming arches. 'Make eight seats, all draped in white,' he told Sumana, 'and strew the floor with flowers and puffed rice. Do all that is necessary, dear wife, for I go to prepare the road upon which the saintly ones will come.' And this they did. Tissa prepared the road, filling all the hollows, clearing and cleaning it and spreading upon it a layer of white sand. He strewed upon it the flowers of the champak and the jasmine, then stood at the end of it, at the entrance to the village, so sure was he that the holy ones would come.'

'And his faith was rewarded, mother,'

'Yes, for such is the power of faith, child.'

Devi sighed. Yes, she would keep faith too, prepare her song, sing it some day to the prince who held her heart.

'In the Talaguru temple in the southern kingdom of Ruhuna, was the sainted elder, the venerable

Dhammadinna,' the mother said, smoothing her daughter's soft black hair, her hand idly caressing the black tresses. 'He was of such goodly character that his was the gift of the spiritual eye,[129] and he saw the great devotion of Tissa and thought to fulfil the craftsman's wish. He went to his own spiritual elder, the holy Godhamma, and said, "O Master, such devotion have my eyes seen. Let us go to the house of Tissa the craftsman, there in the village of Mundavaka by the river, where the alms await us." And the holy Godhamma cast his eye forth, saw the manner of Tissa's preparations and said, "It is good. We will gather six other elders, the holiest of them, and take with us alms bowls." And so did these eight monks come to the village, my child.'

'And they rose in the air from the land of Ruhuna, mother. Like stars all robed in yellow did they come upon the wings of the wind. You did not say that, mother.'

'Yes, that is how they came. And when they descended, each with his robe knotted to the robe of the other, holding their alms bowls, they stood before Tissa just as a row of royal swans would stand in a pond of lotus. That was how they came to Tissa, my child, one behind the other with the senior and wisest of them leading.'

'What joy Tissa must have felt.'

'Overwhelmed was he, for he fell upon his face, prostrate in worship. His hands did shake as he took their bowls, led them along the flower-strewn road, beneath the banana tree arch, into his scented home where the eight seats awaited them. Then did he offer rice gruel and sweets and bade Sumana take away the wrapping from the pot of flesh, heat it again and add to it honey and palm sugar. This, bravely sweetened, did he give to the elders and after this did he offer goodly portions of *suvanda hal* that is the sweet-smelling wild rice whose grains are fragrant when boiled, together with meat and fish.'

'The fragrant rice, oh mother! The fragrant rice! This was the sign of the coming of the prince. The granaries smoked with the scent of the rice within at his birth…'

'Ah, do you then wish to tell the rest of the tale, daughter? There is little left to tell.'

'No, no. This is the part I love to hear. Oh, what a song I will make of this. Say on, mother.'

'This rice of fragrant grain…yes, a wonder surely. It is thought that the arahats who received the alms, by their wondrous merits, made the rice so fragrant. And so noble a sermon of thanksgiving did they preach before they returned with miraculous ease to their temples in Ruhuna. And thereafter did Tissa increase ever in goodness. So good a man did he become that the chief monks of many temples who had heard of his meritorious deeds, declared that he would be reborn a prince of the realm.'

'And so it was, mother.'

'Hush, child. Say not so outside these walls. Many there are who say that the good Tissa has returned in this present life as the son of our great king, but who could be certain?'

'Then the rice, mother? The fragrant rice?'

'People say much, but is it just the rice that tells us that the good Tissa has returned as our prince? In our village was an old woman who gathered Asoka flowers as you now do. She would croon over them and rock them in her lap. Is it then said that you are this old woman reborn, because you gather the flowers too?'

Devi pouted. 'Yes, you say true, mother, but many a time I have wished that I were the good Sumana, the wife of the craftsman Tissa, in my last birth…'

Her mother stiffened, clutched at the hair on Devi's head. 'Say no such thing ever again!' she exclaimed.

Devi gave a little cry, twisted away. Her lustrous eyes shone with the hint of tears. 'Mother, what...'

Her mother rose. 'Say no more. See how your flowers wilt. Go now and fill the pots for the night.'

Devi saw the paleness in her mother's face and all but ran to the back of the hut where the buckets stood. In the little kitchen, her mother moved around aimlessly, stopped to look at the flowers, their petals limp. She coughed and ran a hand through her hair. The wife of Tissa, the gentle Sumana, daughter of a craftsman, had also gathered Asoka flowers. Sumanavo was she called when but a headstrong little girl. Sumanavo, who always wore an Asoka flower in her hair...

Carl Muller

Sumanavo

It was in that time of unrest, when the tales of the sweeping might of Duttha Gamani were coursing through the land, that in the region east of the great river, did Nagasena, a potter, took to wife the virtuous Pabavathi. There did they live, where in the distance rose the Niyelatissa[130] and there did they stay in safety and comfort, learning of the defeat and death of Elara and of the rout of the Damilas.

It was when Pabavathi was big with child that she said to her husband, 'So distanced are we from the sacred city. Can we not move there that I may pray at the Bodhi tree and see the great works our king now performs?'

Nagasena thought about this, but was loath to leave. 'There is little room in the city. We will not have such freedom as we have here. I dislike the places where many live, crowded together.'

But Pabavathi would not be denied. She was strong-headed, and wished that the child she carried be born in the city. 'Would you deny me this—this wish I share with our unborn child?' she cried.

The older men of the village told Nagasena, 'You must not deny her in her condition. You are a good craftsman, for you also turn your hand to wood and metal. In the city, you would do well.'

So Nagasena came to the small settlement of Hellioli, outside the inner city of Anuradhapura. The older men had been right. He found much to do, and what was more, his wife was happy. The house they occupied was small, but there was a spacious compound as large as a paddy tract, and it was easy to bring, by means of a little channel that ran from the Malvattu river, the water needed to tend a thriving home garden.

There, he earned the praises of many, for his work in metal was much commented on, and he found more work than he ever had done in his old village. Yet, he would dream of the old days and his eyes would mist over with the pain of remembering. He ached for the placid hours he spent at the margins of the forest where, at times, herds of deer abounded. Wild pigs would root about and he would always hear the loud calls of the green pigeons. There too had he actually seen the elephants at rest, lying upon the ground, their great bulks heaving gently in sleep, hind legs extended backwards, enabling the beasts to draw their feet gradually under them when they needed to rise.[131]

But it was good to be so busy, and naturally it was not long before, as a good craftsman, he was pressed into the service of the court. Many hours of each week did he spend with the other craftsmen, discussing design and embellishment and the preparation and shaping of iron, copper and the pouring of bronze.

Pabavathi bore a daughter, also of the colour of palest bronze, a beautiful child who was the joy of her parents. 'She is as a little devi,' Nagasena said not without pride, and Pabavathi would put her face close to the infant and inhale the warm smell and sigh. 'She is of the scent of sandalwood. We must ask the elders to read the signs of her fate. Bend close, husband. Does her mouth not smell of the water lilies? A good name must we give her.'

The astrologers were of no uncertainty. This child would grow to greatness. 'We see great hopes, unconquerable desires. She will be as a light to be seen and followed and she will live in goodness and grace when she grows up to find her happiness with a master craftsman as her father is.'

Nagasena was pleased. No sons had he but it was good to know that this girl would bring a craftsman into the family. He studied the baby with a new awareness. 'She *is* beautiful, is she not?'

Pabavathi smiled proudly. 'Much distress did she cause me in her bringing forth. I trust she will no longer do so.'

'That is what old women always say,' Nagasena grinned. 'Just look at her. She shines. Truly does she shine. Her spirit shines within her.'

They called her Sumanavo.

It is only now that modern science is compelled to accept reincarnation as a reality. Dharmawardene, of the University of Colombo,[132] has said that reincarnation may be defined as the re-embodiment of an immaterial part of a person after an indetermined period after death, in a new body, wherein it continues to lead a new life, often unconscious of its previous existence. Yet, it contains within itself the essence of the result of its past life or lives, and those experiences of the past go to make up the character and personality of the present.

In presenting his case for reincarnation, Dharmawardene explained how, in the seventeenth century, René Descartes divided everything in the universe into two realms—*res extensa* (matter) and *res cognitans* (mind). Knowledge gathered within the former realm was science: all-important, respectable knowledge, measurable, recognizable and explainable. This dealt with the ultimate realities as things, not beings. Thus the framework of classical science was constructed, bringing with it material benefits, technology and advancement.

The latter realm was regarded as a sort of lunatic fringe, certainly not respectable and quite undignified. But quite perversely, things began to happen that punctured the comfortable cushions of classical armchairs. In 1896, Henry Becquerel discovered radioactivity and later, Einstein propounded his theory of relativity. Then came the quantum theory and the uncertainty principle. None of these resorted to experiment or measurement. There were no objects to be studied, but suddenly, res extensa was forced to look beyond the five senses into murky regions of nature where nothing known applied, and yet, everything known and unknown existed. Mechanisms were no longer the perceptible mental pictures we could understand.

Dharmawardene cited the example of a single electron that could pass through two different holes in a screen at the same time and still remain a single particle on the other side. Where was absolute precision? So came modern science, and with it the understanding that the two realms could not stand arbitrarily on their own, that they were actually one. Classical science and religious bias and other factors had refused to accept the truths of the unknown, but it is different today. Modern science can now bypass old-time bias, taboos and restrictions, to investigate such phenomena as rebirth, re-becoming and reincarnation. Even Descartes, despite his unswerving faith in res extensa, confirmed his belief in life after death when in 1641, he wrote:

> What I have said is sufficient to show, clearly enough, that the extinction of the mind does not follow from the corruption of the body, and also to give men the hope of another life after death.

Even as the writer will go on to tell of the many soul passages or spirit journeys of those of this chapter, allow me to remind readers that this work unquestionably accepts the voyages of the spirit as told in the Chronicles and of the faith of this resplendent land. We have already seen how king Duttha Gamani himself was none other than a holy samanera whose death wish was to be born again in the womb of Vihara Maha Devi.[133]

In the reincarnation scenario, infancy brings back a scroll inscribed with ancestral histories that stretch back to a dim, cloudy past. The immaterial part of the body returns, reappears after a period spent in a scientifically unknown state. Today, with research, hypnosis and 'past life therapy' there is a strong conviction that all human capabilities could be extended beyond birth to a previous life and beyond. It has even been seen how phobias that attend present life are linked directly with the manner of death or disaster experienced in the past. Even Cicero determined that the speed with which children grasp innumerable facts is strong proof of them knowing of such before birth...and always the belief came to hold ground that that prodigy, precocious talent, genius, is really a flowering of past life.

As Austrian scientist Rudolf Steiner had said:

> Just as an age was once ready to receive the Copernican theory of the universe, so is our age ready for the idea of

reincarnation to be brought into the general consciousness of humanity.

It must be said that in the times of Duttha Gamani and for millennia earlier, the realm of res cognitans was of equal strength to that of the practicalities of scientific endeavour. That is why the writer asks that we be mindful of such, as you are told of the girl called Sumanavo—for here is a tale of lives without end, each growing, glowing, until in beauty, in poverty, in humility, in goodness, they take their reward in the loving arms of a prince.

Pabavathi loved to spend her forenoons at the bodhi tree. She would take little Sumanavo, who would chatter like a very noisy sparrow, and she would not fail to take flowers in a lotus-leaf wrapping, and a new pot Sumanavo would dart away to the side of the road to exclaim at the swarms of white butterflies that rose around the banks of white and pink *galkaranda*[134] or stop to gaze at the wreaths of pink wax flowers[135] that rioted upon the branches of the Indian laburnum.[136]

Pabavathi would tell her daughter of the bodhi tree and how the *deva putra*[137] Apratihatanetra was one of the sixteen guardians of the Bodhi Mandala.[138] She wanted Sumanavo to know of the greatness of the faith and of those stirring times when the south branch of the sacred tree came to Lanka, attended by many miracles.[139]

'See child, there is the Upasika vihara where the holy Sanghamitta dwelt. It was built by the great king Devanampiya Tissa, and there did Sanghamitta reside with her companions. And do you see that other dwelling? There...yes, that dwelling. I will take you there soon. That,

Carl Muller

too, is a nunnery—a place built by Sanghamitta who, I told you, was the daughter of the emperor of Jambudvipa, the noble Asoka. Yes, I must take you there. You know its name? It is called the Aritthathapitagara...'

'Arittha...thata...' little Sumanavo laughed delightedly. 'What a long name that is.'

Her mother smiled. 'Don't skip around so. Your feet are red with the dust. Now listen...It is called so because therein is enshrined the *arittha*[140] of the ship on which Sanghamitta came to this land, the ship that brought the holy tree.'[141]

Many were the stories told, and much did little Sumanavo learn as they made their preparations around the bodhi tree. Pabavathi would always sweep away the litter around the tree, lovingly gathering every fallen leaf, depositing them on the offerings slab. Sumanavo would gather the litter and carry it beyond the borders of the sacred area, return to watch her mother light the joss sticks and lay the flowers. She always liked to place the flowers, all buttery and creamy, some of startling red and others of the colour of melting gold. 'Know you child how the king's chief minister went to the emperor's court in Pataliputta, to bring back Sanghamitta and this tree...He was Maha Arittherha. A good man, and nephew of the king. So noble was he that Asoka made him a senapati[142] and when he returned to Lanka, he became a bhikkhu. Imagine that. It is told how a great *sangiti*[143] was held in the refuge of the minister Meghavannabhaya at the Thuparama. Even the holy Mahinda came to this recital, my child.'[144]

It would be not in the least possible to say that a six-year-old remained dutifully at her mother's side while the good woman went about her devotions. Also, Pabavathi never took her daughter to the little channel, when she went to fill her pot. 'Wait here and think upon what I have told you, daughter. I will be back in a little while.'

Sumanavo would pout prettily. She had stuck little stalks of flowering grass in her hair and drew up her knees, pulling her cloth down around her shins. She liked the little rivulet that ran, all sun-shot, along the western boundary of the Maha Vihara. The trees drooped heavy-leaved branches and the grass was cool. She looked around, listened to the susurration of the bo leaves. It was hot, and she was hungry. Rising, she looked towards the path her mother had taken, then with a small exclamation of impatience, ran home, brushing at the hair that fell over her face. She knew the road well, and, as she later said, she was hot and hungry—and her father patted her head although he did say that she was a bad girl. She ran indoors and the pot of rice congee on the hearth looked most inviting. Quickly, she served herself a portion in a bowl, spilling much on the hearthstones. The bench she perched on rocked as she climbed down, and the ladle fell on the floor. Bending to retrieve it, she tipped over most of the gruel, tried to sweep it away with her foot and spread the soft grains, all mushy, over the graying brick. She stared at the mess, then began to eat hurriedly. She would first take away the pinch in her stomach and then tidy the little kitchen. After all, she was only a little girl, was she not? Her mother should have been here to give her food.

It was to this scene that Pabavathi came, slightly breathless through hurrying, worried that her child was not at the Bodhi tree. Her relief on finding Sumanavo at home was soon dispelled on seeing the mess in her kitchen. 'Look at you!' she cried. 'Have you fed the floor also? Why did you not stay as I told you to?'

'But I was hungry...'

'Quiet! Look at the floor...and the fireplace? Is this how you eat? Like a chandala girl? Yes, that is what you are...a chandala girl!'

Sumanavo paled, burst into tears. 'I am not a chandala girl. It is you who are a chandala girl.'

Pabavathi's anger flamed. 'So now you abuse your mother, do you?' She wrenched the bowl from her daughter's hands, flung it away. 'Leave my kitchen! Go and wash yourself!'

Sumanavo sobbed when her father returned. 'I did not mean what I said,' she pleaded, and she felt his hand kindly pat her head.

'But you scolded your mother, little one. See, she is no longer angry, for this that you said will you be punished some day...'

She fell asleep that night to the sweet singing of her mother. Yes, she was no longer angry, and always sang to her.

Sumanavo was not destined to live past her girlhood. She had, as her parents knew, a nature that brooked neither advice nor interference. She would skip outdoors to where the Asoka trees grew, romp in the fields to the east and splash in the puddles that lay between tall grasses after rain. And she never forgot that afternoon when her mother had berated her. Suddenly, she began to sicken, grow leaner, paler. Her father went to the astrologers.

'You have said that she would bring a craftsman into our family,' he reminded, 'yet the priest says she has a wasting disease. Is it that she will recover?'

The wise men shook their heads. 'We read the signs of her birth and made no mistake. But born she was in the time of the rising of the dragon that swallows the sun. Thus could we not say in what existence would this truly come to pass. The signs are correct, O Nagasena. She will marry a craftsman, but perhaps it would occur in an afterlife.'

'You mean…'

'Aye. Even in her next life or the next. But it will come to pass. That must she fulfil.'

'But she seems close to death even now.'

'It is in the hands of the celestial ones.'

So did Sumanavo die, and if the astrologers spoke true, there was born, in the village of Mundavaka, a daughter to a craftsman who was kin to Nagasena of Hellioli. It was with some effort that the grieving Nagasena and Pabavathi journeyed to Mundavaka. The little house was adorned with an arch of tender coconut fronds and Nagasena's kinsman and wife received them with gentle words, knowing that the hurt of loss was still fresh in them.

'We have brought a gift for the little one,' said Pabavathi.

'We thank you,' the mother said. 'Will you look on our daughter?'

They gazed at the infant and their tears flowed freely. They were looking at *their* daughter, surely! The same beautiful soft-haired girl they had been blessed with twelve years ago. Pabavathi could scarce control herself. 'My little Sumanavo,' she cried, taking the child fiercely to her bosom.

'Not Sumanavo, cousin sister,' the father said. 'We have called her Sumana. So beautiful a daughter is she not?'

'Nay, cousin brother,' Nagasena said, his voice shaking. 'This is our Sumanavo. Truly she is. Born again to you, brother. Our daughter and yours.'

To the people of Mundavaka, this was neither strange nor wonderful. Life, they knew, never disappeared into some place of no return. Sumanavo or Sumana, this new life

Carl Muller

grew to capture the heart of the craftsman Tissa, bringing into the family, as the astrologers had said, another fine worker in metal, wood and clay.

It would not be necessary to recount the events already told of—of the alms-giving to the monks of the Ruhuna temples, of the virtuous lives of Tissa and Sumana. Their cords of life were not snapped even as they passed away, for Tissa was to be reborn the son of Duttha Gamani, and Sumana to return as the daughter of the chandala chief of the settlement at Hellioli, that, as we return to the present, was the settlement of the city's outcastes.

How true it was that Sumanavo would be punished some day in her lifetime or another, for taunting her mother, calling her a chandala girl. Her punishment, said the seers, was so evident. She was, two incarnations later, Sumana Devi, a chandala maid! And so much did she carry within her in her new life—the sweet voice of her previous mother, Pabavathi, a beauty that shone, that dazzled so that it was said there was no need to light a lamp in a room she was in. Her body light, people said, spread on all sides for a distance of four cubits. And in her heart, even as she gathered the Asoka flowers and sang and dreamed of a happiness yet to come, was the need to find once again, the love of Tissa, her husband of Mundavaka, when she was his Sumana in her previous birth.

Is it any wonder that prince Saliya, a lover of the craftsman's art (for was he not the craftsman Tissa) should be stirred to love, be so captivated by the chandala maid? He had found again the beauteous wife of his previous existence. He would do anything to make her his...give up anything...even the lion throne!

❖

Ariyapala[145] tells us that social and psychological problems played a vital role in marriage in those times. Children who contemplate marriage on their own accord faced the wrath of their parents, fear of disinheritance, loss of love, family prestige, status and wealth. Marriage was considered best according to orthodox family tradition.

Meyer[146] tells us that the same pattern was true of India and reminds us of the words of Bhisma to Yudhisthira in the Mahabharatha:

> The good must give the daughter to a wooer gifted with excellencies, having informed themselves of his character and way of life, his knowledge, his origin and his business.

The Pancatantra asks that the wise give their daughters to one endowed with the qualities of caste, family, character, protection, learning, wealth or power, beauty, health and youth.[147]

Love did not really come into all this but, as we see, it did matter, but was always considered an exception in the normal course of events, where marriages were arranged by the parents of both parties. The *Saddharmaratnavaliya* gives us many stories of how caste, like standing and profession, played an important part in marriage. However, when love stepped in, all such considerations were tossed aside and we read of abductions and elopements and instances where women fell in love with robbers and even servants of their households.

Also, it was held true that no man would directly propose to a woman unless he was in love with her. Whatever the times, be it 500 BC or AD 100 there was also the general acceptance that, be they ever so well educated and well versed in the arts and crafts, women were lower than men and also full of feminine wiles and of a more evil nature. This general assumption did not include such popularly loved and venerated women as Vihara Maha Devi, but the writing of the times and later did cast women in a most unfavourable light. The *Saddharmalankaraya*[148] consider women as deceivers and delusions:

> They cannot be relied upon, they are like a mirage. They are a mine of danger, sorrow and illness. They are like snares laid by Mara to capture passionate men, like a cave of bears, like a door of the cave of Mara...

It goes on to say:

> They are never satisfied with the number of men they have; they make no distinction of caste and creed. Their thirst for sensual pleasure, ornament and decoration can never be satiated.

The *Saddharmaratnavaliya*[149] shares like views. We are told that:

> ...women are like places for drawing water... just as the haunts of drunkards and watering places are common to all and are not for one and only one individual, similarly women belong to everyone irrespective of caste, creed or social status. They are counsellors to birth in Purgatory... women are the cause of all ills, and embrace men for their own gains, just as the creepers the trees for their own support.

It seems quite extraordinary that such has been said and written in those far-off times, and such sentiments are echoed in other writings too. The *Kavsilumina*[150] describes women as:

> ... a festival to the five senses, whirlpools in the ocean of life, a tap root of the creeper of craving, a door open to Purgatory...

The *Pujavaliya*[151] declares:

It is the universal nature of women to see the beauty of other women and wish that they were as beautiful; to see the heroic deeds of a man and wish that he were her husband; to see the caresses of another's child and wish the child were hers.

Of course, most of these old texts were written by pious men and contained admonitions for those who followed the austere life. To such—monks and ascetics—women needed to be viewed with a certain repugnance. It is true that these works propounded ethics: the right practice of which the authors sought to inculcate by means of their works. The *Saddharmalankaraya*, for example, accurately reflects the author–monk's didactic intentions. We must remember that Buddhist ethics are based on two fundamentals: the law that individual beings are born not once, but many times over in various forms and in various worlds. Thus can they be human, subhuman, suprahuman, animal, spirit or god. The other is the causal connection between actions in one birth and circumstances and events of life in a subsequent birth.

The *Pujavaliya*, also written by a monk, gives us, perversely enough, long accounts of the physical beauties of women, while the *Saddharmaratnavaliya*, also written by a monk, extols the virtuous life and gives us a graphic account of how a courtesan attempted to seduce a monk:

She laughed loudly and looked at his face. She swayed her hips, uncovered her thighs ad covered them again. She put aside her upper garment and exposed her breasts. She raised her arm and displayed her armpit. She buried the pupils of her eyes, raised her eyebrows, put out her tongue and licked her lips. She loosened her garments and tightened them again. She loosened her hair and tied it up again.

The *Kavsilumina*, as tradition would have it, was composed by King Parakrama Bahu II (1234–69) and is a very ornate poem. Again, it dwells on the pleasures of the senses and waxes eloquent on the manner in which the king conducts his sensual revels in his drinking chamber.

What may be best to bear in mind is that, whatever the age, a king could still look upon a vision of loveliness and declare (as has been declared in folk tale): 'This beggar maid shall be my queen!' Love has this habit of conquering all, despite all the pious strictures this world has known. And is it any wonder, then, that a loving husband and wife of a previous birth should gravitate towards each other in their present incarnation?

A weary courier clattered up to the inner gates and all but slumped off his horse. 'A *hasun*—a written message from the queen,' he said, 'for the king.'

Duttha Gamani received the messenger eagerly. 'And is the queen well and has she been received in a fitting manner?'

'All of the south pour forth their love, sire. Ruhuna is festive as never before.'

Duttha Gamani broke the seal, read the scroll. 'Make of our prince Saliya a viceroy. It is time that he be elevated in his journey to kingship. A fitting palace must he occupy. This do we wish more than all else.'

He frowned. 'Now—at this time…this concern for our son,' he muttered. He lowered the scroll. 'Tell us, how does the queen seem? Have you seen her in good health and spirit?'

'That I did, sire.'

The king's brow cleared. He thought he had sensed a feeling of haste in is mother's wish, but he did accept that it was time his son accepted the responsibilities of governance and finally, as his mother said, kingship. 'You will carry back our reply tomorrow,' he said and picked up the scroll as he courier bowed himself out. 'Surely our mother will wish to be here at the ceremony of elevation,' he thought. 'We will ask that she returns.'

Carl Muller

A Question Of Succession

VIHARA MAHA DEVI SHOOK HER HEAD. A SAD LITTLE GESTURE, Tissa thought, and felt concern. 'But our mother,' he said, 'would not our king be pained that you are not in attendance for the prince's great hour? Surely are we glad for the prince. It is right, is it not, that he succeeds to the throne?'

'Yes, it is right. Saliya is a fine young man and is well loved by all. And kingship is hereditary. But there has been this rule, our son, and thus did our brother promise Rajarata to you.'

Tissa laughed. 'Our brother could not know at that time that he would father so fair a son. I count not the fingers of the hand that gives. Look around you. This is your realm too, is it not? How real is the love our people have shown you. And many are our sons too, and yet, there will be no queen of Ruhuna save you. Is this not truly where you belong?'

Vihara Maha Devi smiled.

'We think you must return as the king asks of you. We must go, for it will be considered strange that we do not.'

'You are right. The people too will think it strange. But the preparations for such a ceremony will take time.

117

I will ask that we be given a date, and then shall we go some days ahead.'

Tissa was relieved. He felt that his mother was finding the many demands on her a strain. She wished, more and more, to spend her time as it pleased her, going where she wished unheralded, free of ceremony and trappings. It came upon him suddenly. His mother was feeling her years. She was old! Her life had burned fiercely, over-bright. Had there come a dimness? He touched her hand fondly. 'This is for you the quiet time, is it not?'

Her eyes, as she regarded him, were luminous and he saw the love in them and was unnerved. 'Mother, what is it?'

'We must go to all the places of the past,' she said. 'To all the places that filled our lives so, see them again, know them and understand how they have touched us. Yes, that must we now do before we return.'

'Places? You wish to travel? But these journeyings tire you so. Is it wise?'

She didn't seem to hear him. Her mind was wandering far, ranging the kingdoms, the hills, the lush plains, the rocky heights. Suddenly, her forehead creased as if in pain. 'And you, too, will be king of all Lanka, our son. You too.'

The *Vishnu Purana* gives us an idea of the dynasties of kings as recorded by the Hindus. There have been occasions, as the writer will later record, when princes and even senapatis slew the ruling king to seize the throne, but as always, kingship was hereditary. In his translation of the *Culavamsa*[152] Geiger declared:

Carl Muller

...as to the right of succession, the rule was that the very youngest brother of the king succeeded him on the throne. Only when no other brother existed did the crown pass to the next generation, and here again, to the eldest son of the eldest brother of the preceding generation.

Ariyapala[153] contests this, claiming that this may have been the practice in particular cases, but always the succession passed from father to son.

It is best to remember that such succession was the general rule in India as well, and there was no real reason for the Aryans to change or deviate from it. Law[154] summed up the Indian tradition as follows:

The selection of the eldest son as successor to the kingdom appears to have been the normal mode of disposition in ancient times. The ruling of a kingdom by brothers in rotation has, as far as we see, nowhere been recorded as having taken place in the dominions of the Solar and Lunar kings in ancient times.

We also find strong support in the *Saddharmaratnavaliya*[155] and the *Saddharmalankaraya*.[156] The former states: 'The son succeeds to the father's kingdom' while the latter tells of a son 'being honoured with the office of sub-king... engaged himself in all duties of kingship after the death of his father.'

One thing must be said however. We will soon see how the community of monks also exercised their powers to choose a king. The ministers also had their say in such election, where an elder son is ignored and a younger placed on the throne. It is obvious that the Sangha had a chief voice in the selection of a king, and claimed the right to elect a prince of their choosing in order that such king remain, at all times, the sole guardian of the Buddhist faith and doctrine.

Thus, a prince could not simply step into his father's shoes merely by right. It was necessary, according to the Sangha, that this successor possesses the necessary qualifications. This, too was a custom in pre-Buddhist India, and Mehta[157] says:

> ...we have instances which show that heredity was often not the sole support by which a prince could get on to the throne. He was thoroughly examined by ministers and, if found worthy and capable, then only was he declared fit for kingship.

We also find this position summed up for us by Dharma[158] who, while conceding that kings were hereditary as a rule, noted that new kings could not succeed as a matter of right; and had to be formerly elected by a peoples' assembly:

> Although kings succeeded one another by the law of primogeniture, where the eldest son succeeded to the throne of the father, the successor could also be disqualified as unfitting or unworthy and a younger son elevated by virtue of his qualifications, education, etc. Consent and approval was necessary before a king could be crowned.

Even Codrington[159] said that 'where the succession was doubtful, the selection of the new monarch in practice, lay with the principal ministers'.

Hayley[160] added that:

> In theory, the sovereign was elected by the people, and the tradition of the right to choose or approve of the prince nominated to succeed appears to have survived even the tyrannies established by the last occupants of the throne.

Duttha Gamani had a choice. Even as he marched out of Magama, leading his forces against the Damilas, he had given his brother kingship over Ruhuna and a promise that someday Tissa would be monarch of all Lanka. But prince Saliya was well loved and the monks minded not that the prince succeed. 'It is the natural thing, O king,' they had said, 'and truly is the prince loved and admired by all.'

'Too well admired, if we may say so,' Duttha Gamani said, 'for his form and features draw many to him.'

The chief priest had nodded. 'We have noted this too, but now, grown to manhood, is he his own man. Delicate of taste is he and well nurtured in the arts, and yet, does he fulfil his duties with a manly bearing. A good and acceptable king will he be.'

Duttha Gamani was pleased at the monk's words. Saliya would be first a viceroy, and even now was a splendid palace being built for him in the southern quarter. There would be a complete ceremony of inauguration with all rites and rituals.

'But lord, it is necessary, for such a ritual, that the prince has as his consort a Kshatriya maiden,' the chief of the council said.

'Surely that is demanded of a king, not a viceroy.'

'To that extent yes, lord king, but you give to the prince the principality of the south where he will be as king. Is it not thy wish that even the taxes of the people of the southern district be paid to the prince?'

'And is that not befitting his state? To be as king is the way in which he will learn and know all that would make him the acceptable king. Know you this: we wish that this ceremony be as the ritual of kingly consecration. The prince will be a kingly viceroy, a kingly uparaja and, on ascending to the lion throne, a king of kings. What? Do we not wish that our successor be the noblest in the land?'

The preparations demanded, as the wise men sought, three chanks and water from the Ganges. A royal chair needed to be positioned in a special pavilion—a pavilion that had to be specially constructed in the centre of the main hall of the southern palace. The sea chanks had to be spiralled right and Duttha Gamani wished that the shells be embellished with silver. 'Let the turban also be of cloth of silver and silver rainment must he wear. The astrologers have deemed it so.'

All this had given cause for much comment among the elders of the council. 'Scarlet and gold, and always is the turban threaded with purple,' one said. 'Is it that the king wishes the prince to be viceroy only?'

'Nay, for the prince is named successor.'

'Then why silver? Even the chanks are inlaid with silver. Should not one at least be gilded?'

'He follows not the ritual of consecration. I feel he wishes to dilute the ceremony.'

'To what purpose?'

'Well…that the prince will be successor we are certain… methinks he seeks to school the prince in the ways of a king. Thus will there be a semblance of a ceremony and we will have a king of the southern quarter who is not a king. And yet, will he be as a king and rule the south. It is an imposition of discipline, to be sure.'

'I feel that the prince is too weak, too—too soft, and too—too…'

'Softly, old man. He was but a boy no long ago. He looks upon his duties with care and diligence now.'

Krishnacharya and Venkobacharya[161] laid down the articles necessary for the consecration of a king. While it is necessary to repeat that the elevation of Prince Saliya to the status of sub-king did not call for the full paraphernalia of consecration, it is interesting to know how well Duttha Gamani 'diluted' the ritual, acting on the advice of his wise men and astrologers. Even as the preparations were completed, the astrologers shook perplexed heads. The signs spoke of shifting directions. Ascending in the south, there would be a movement westward and then, just as the moon plunges behind cloud, would the light be dimmed. They reread the horoscope. They were agreed on one thing. Whatever the ceremonial, Saliya would not be king, would not sit in the lion seat of his father.

Yet, the preparations were made. The golden water vessels, the palanquin spread with the skin of a leopard, gold and silver urns which would hold the white lotuses, the silver-skin umbrella. Honey, milk, curd and ghee would be needed, together with parched grain. A young elephant would be permitted to wander around the palace and in the courtyard would a white heifer be tethered as well as a white steed. Eight maidens garbed in scarlet and silver would scatter eight varieties of flowers and the musical instruments would also be of silver, even the drums rimmed with the precious metal.

It was significant that Duttha Gamani wished a silver umbrella. Indeed the holy men had asked that silver be the dominant colour. 'The element of water is of the attributes of the prince,' they said, 'and to this is added the element of air in quantity. Silver is the propitious colour.'

It has always been necessary that an umbrella and fan be part of the necessary articles for any royal inauguration. The special pasada, pavilion, in which the ceremony is held is also part of the custom of a high festival. The sacred water, sprinkled on the head of the personage so elevated, was the first part of the ceremony. In the *Aitareya Brahmana* of the Rig Veda[162] we are told that the principal part of all such ceremonies consists in the sprinkling of holy water over the heads (of kings). The ceremonial chair has to be of Udumbara wood[163] and the Jatakas[164] state:

> The king was seated in a fine chair of udumbara wood and was sprinkled with auspicious water from a conch with spirals turned rightwise.[165]

That Prince Saliya was to wear a turban was also significant. There would be no crown or diadem. He would be, as Duttha Gamani wished, a 'rising king' yet no king. Indeed, the crown was never considered of real importance save to be symbolically worn, then put aside. Even in ancient India there was little reference to a coronation. The ceremony was of *abhiseka*[166] and the crowning a mere gesture. Even the Mahabharatha,[167] when describing the consecration of Yudhisthira, makes no reference to a crown. The edicts of Asoka[168] also refer to anointing and not to a coronation, and this held true even during the age of of the Guptas.[169] Many writers have, in using the term 'coronation' given the impression that the crown was the crucial symbol of the ceremony, losing sight of the word abhiseka or *abhisimcismu*. We find this evident in the *Saddharmaratnavaliya* where the phrase 'sprinkled water' has been replaced by 'the placing of the crown'.

Carl Muller

The fact that Duttha Gamani ignored the necessity of a consort tells us that Saliya was not to be regarded as true king. The *Mahavamsa* says that Panduvasdeva was given the sovereignty of Lanka but, since he had no consort, was not solemnly consecrated. Duttha Gamani wished that his mother was with him. He needed to consult with her and he found it hard to take so many important decisions without hearing of her views and feelings. It was necessary that the prince had a consort or that a fitting maiden be chosen, ready to be his queen at the appropriate time. He had asked of Saliya: 'Is there no one you esteem among the noble maidens?' and had seen the colour rise in his son's cheeks. Saliya had dropped his gaze, remained silent.

'Lo, we will have much to concern ourselves when the Maha Thupa is raised. Yet, in this time of waiting, we wish to see you take the reins into your own hands.' He thought awhile. 'A princess must you have. We will talk of this when our mother returns.'

The *Saddharmalankaraya* tells us much of Prince Saliya. This work, by Devarakshita Jayabahu Dharmakirti, was written in the fourteenth century, and the title, that may be reflected in English as 'The Ornament of the Good Law' reflects the author's didactic intentions. While it is solely to depict the lives of the pious, showing how well the 'good law' works, it is also important to understand that the author–monk found, in Saliya, how well this law worked. The following passage from this work fixes the popular idea of what the prince was even as a good and kindly youth:

This fortunate prince grew up in glorious prosperity. He had the beautiful appearance of one who has performed many virtuous deeds in former lives. He was a source of delight to all of those who looked upon him. He bore himself majestically and his royal power was boundless. He was mature in prowess. His fame spread in all the ten directions. His understanding was always perfectly suited to the occasion. His form was a joy to behold. His speech was sweet to the ear. He knew the truth which does not change. He neither feared nor trembled. In his generosity he was like a wish-conferring tree. As to wealth, he was like a vast treasure house. In strength he was like Bala Deva, the brother of Krishna. To all beings he was as a mother. His wish to give alms was insatiable. Daily in the morning, gods and men brought presents to him worth a thousand coins, but before noon he would give away everything that had been brought. In the afternoon he was brought presents worth five hundred coins, but he would give it all to the beggars keeping nothing to himself. He sought refuge only in the Three Gems.[170]

This is an exceedingly romanticized idea, but it does confirm many of the traits of young Saliya—beautiful and effeminate to a marked degree, a lover of beauty. He attracted many, both men and women, and he did not spare himself in his desire to give, even his body, to those who told him of their love, their need of him, even those who made of him an object of their lust and passion. Fondled, caressesd, loved, seeking love where he could, his artistic sensitivities held him bound to his own dark passivity. He would not, could not, turn his face from any who declared their need of him. He asked more and more for the embrace of the men who used him, men and even older boys who learned that this strange youth wanted gentleness, tenderness, and who yielded to them just as any woman would, thrilling to the soft promise of a lover's caress. And he had seen the chandala maid and he knew of a love so blinding that he was drowning himself in a sea of desire. Suddenly, he was all man. Suddenly, he was a prince—a prince who would also be a king; and a king who would need in his bed the only woman who had been his, beyond the memory of this, his present life.

He was happy to learn that Vihara Maha Devi would return. He had always loved her, admired her, wondered at the stories, the epic of her life. But he remained aloof too, for his melting nature made him wary of so heroic a woman. She could be hard, bold, decisive and determined. Why, he thought, she could be a man in so many ways, and he saw how much store his father laid in her. 'My grandmother is queen,' he muttered, 'and my father is king, and I am a prince and will be a king. And who then is my true mother?'

This had been one of the driving circumstances of his boyhood and youth. Loved so well by all, yet denied the natural love of his mother. What was love anyway? The stone carver of Issarama had loved him so much in that grey-walled cave. Long hours of touching, pressing, the lean fingers making him so hard, so urgent. He would clutch at the man fiercely, breathing hard at the release of his seed. This was love, surely, this exquisite vomit of sperm that made him throb ecstatically. But now there was a girl, a girl with the eyes of a startled doe, lips like warm rubies, hair that was as a river of ink, and a skin that was melting bronze and gold. He knew then that he would give no more but take. He wanted her so much, this low-caste girl with her angel songs. He could not go to the parkland any more. His teachers surrounded him; he was hemmed in by the many who wished to teach him how to be king. He had much to learn and no time to range the city, walk in the Asoka grove, lie in wait for the girl who had stolen his heart.

❖

It is of relevance to consider that even as these lines are written, the island of Sri Lanka was 'devolved'—a fragmentation of nine regions according to provincial lines, with deplorable vistas of more government, more politicization of decision making, an intensification of the culture of patronage and even revenge, more corruption and very often more social unrest as people became aware of the barriers, both political and psychological.

We find at the juncture of our story, the 'kingdoms' of Ruhuna and the Rajarata of Anuradhapura, as well as the Kalyani territory and the northern peninsula. Also, there lie the central hills and the eastern littoral where, as *Children of the Lion* told, Dighahamini 'ruled' as an eastern 'king'. It is strange to think that despite the presence of an overlord, an emperor, a king who would always claim sovereignty over the whole island, there was little influence such a king could bring to bear upon the territories of other 'kings' and 'princes' who ruled their territories as absolute monarchs and merely acknowledged the emperor by the sending of an annual tribute.

Family ties did much to effect a bonding, and there was no reason to doubt the close and loving relationship between the Rajarata and Ruhuna, where brothers ruled and acknowledged their mother as queen of both kingdoms. Yet, it would be best at this stage to look ahead and examine, in the passage of the centuries, what has always been a Sihala setback. Unity was a most nebulous thing. Kings ruled in many parts of the island and always was there a sense of self-imposition and individualism that brought no good to the land. Divisions were rife, and divisions were always scary. In Sri Lanka today, many politicians sneer at the British colonialists and their need to 'divide and rule'. Yet, the Sinhalese seemed to favour this most of all. Division has spawned monstrous ills and sadly, the lessons have not been learnt. On this day, the first of September 2011, as these lines are written, the move to divide is once more upon us. A sorry move, we feel, but it seems as though Sri Lanka cannot escape the legacy of history!

In 1560, the Spanish cartographer, Cyprian Sanchez, gave us a map of this island showing nine principalities. The peninsula of Jaffna was under a sub-king and the emperor ruled from Kotte, close to Colombo. This map was rendered during the Portuguese era, and the nine principalities were given as:

Imperio de Cotta—*Imperial King of Kotte*
Reino de Ceitaabaha—*Ruler of Sitawaka*
Reino de Canadea—*Ruler of Kandy*
Reino de Jaffnapatam—*Ruler of Jaffna*
Reino de Setra Gorales—*Ruler of Seven Korales*
Chilao Reina—*Ruler of Chilaw*
Reino de Triquilemale—*Ruler of Trincomalee*
Reino de Batticalou—*Ruler of Batticaloa*
Reino de Yala—*Ruler of Yala*[171]

This 1560 map was held among the records of the Catholic Bishop of Goa, who made a voyage to the Portuguese Indies accompanied by Johannes Bugo Linschten. They confirmed that there were nine principalities in Ceylon, the most powerful being Cotta, and identified the principalities of Jaffna, Trincomalee, Batticaloa, Wellasa[172] (which they called Vilassen), Denavaka[173] (called Tenanaka), Yala (called Laula), Kandy and Galle.

The Portuguese historian Queyroz[174] stated that:

> ...after the city of Cota became a metropolis, there were
> 15 kinglets subject to the king of Cota, who therefore was
> considered to be emperor and the same title is as in the
> days claimed by the kings of Kandy subsequently.

Always have the divisions existed and always have such divisions brought grief. As we have seen so far, only two kingdoms stood, joined by brotherly love, at the time of Duttha Gamani. Anuradhapura, as the capital, threw its net of influence over the whole island. The northern province bowed to the Rajarata and so did all of the northern islands. In the east too, and along the western coast did both the Rajarata and Ruhuna exert influence. Yes, even as Vihara Maha Devi decided to go about her beloved land, there was a unity that flamed brightly. Lanka was a true Sihala land, proud and at peace. The times ahead will be told of with infinite sadness, for this great period will surely pass and the old serpent of division will once again raise its head, stare venomously with puffed hood.

No thought of the fiercely corrosive future did Vihara Maha Devi envision as she fared forth. This would be her final odyssey and she would drink deep of this land of much promise, of indescribable beauty. Her son, Tissa, so well loved by all, so acclaimed that he was called Saddha Tissa, the peaceful one, was concerned. 'Hasten back, dear mother, for must we not return to the holy city where the prince will be honoured?'

'We will. We will all do him honour. Wasn't this my wish?'

Saddha Tissa watched the party move away. He had

insisted that his mother be borne in state, in a royal palanquin and she had not demurred. 'And where will you go?' he had asked. 'I will send riders who will bring me daily reports of your movements, and an armed escort. Do not frown so. You are in my care.'

Vihara Maha Devi had smiled. 'For long have we remained here, and before that in Kalyani. Then did we follow the war road to Anuradhapura. So many places are there that we have not looked upon, both east and west. We would see them all if we could. And there is time, for the palace of the prince must first be completed and the propitious time of his elevation has not been as yet declared.'

Tissa had sighed. 'The paths you seek are unfrequented and wild but my men will protect you. Many ox carts of food will follow and all comforts will you have. What more is needed? You have only to tell us.'

She had shaken her head. 'Come, and receive a mother's blessing. It is good that you give us swift riders, for always will I send some of them to the temples that we may spend our nights in the holy places. Ah yes, largesse…and offerings to the monks. Let there be one cart filled with such.'

Tissa had been relieved. His mother was surely taking the pilgrim path and the viharas would be her nightly refuge. He was even happy to think that she would strike east. He had done much in the east and she would be impressed by it all. He had summoned the council. 'The queen journeys at sun-up on the morrow, east, beyond the Menik Ganga. Let all know and prepare for her arrival, even up to the ports of the north-east, aye, even to Gonagama.'[175]

'Gonagama, O king?'

'Yes. The queen goes to the east. Surely will she traverse the pilgrim path.'

The councillors bowed. The *pada yatra*,[176] one said. 'It is a path of many perils.'

'Perils bother her not. What perils did she fear on the path of conquest? She went then to satisfy her blood. Now does she go to satisfy her spirit. See that all is in place to make of this her great journey of spirit.'

The flower altar of the four guardians had been raised in the dawn light. It was to ensure the protection and well-being of the queen in every direction she would travel. The four gods of the east, south, west and north would ensure that Vihara Maha Devi had peaceful passage. The custodian of the Skanda shrine had wished that Tissa make the offering of the flower altar for surely, he said, would the queen traverse the ancient pilgrim way which so many of the faithful tread, their feet scorching in the hot, sandy terrain, in the parched months, as they made their way to the jungle shrine of Kataragama. Who would say no to the thousands that walked—walked from the many villages and townships of India to the coast, sailed the grey-blue waters to Gonagama, then trudged with seeming tirelessness to the south. Always the devotees, the penitents, followed the burning coastal paths to Pannikancherni, Mankerni, Batticaloa, Sinnamuattavaram, Pottuvil, Kumana, their cries rising ecstatically as they approached the fane of the god. They would carry, in clay and brass pots, the water of the sacred Ganges, drawn at Benares, and even the women would carry their pots of holy water slung upon bamboos. A long, excruciating journey of 226 miles. The gentle bays, the Passikudah lagoon would offer them relief, and the breeze would cool them and the waters ease the pain of their blistered feet.

Carl Muller

Of old, the four guardians were Kihiraeli, Saman, Boksael and Vibishana, sprung from the days of the Ramayana. Kihiraeli was Vishnu then; but with the rising of the Kalyani kingdom and the changing times, the gods Tissa laid flowers for were Nata Deva, Vishnu, Skanda or Kataragama Deva, and Pattini. To this day, these are the guardians who are said to have accepted the charge of protecting Lanka.

Nata Deva is said to reside in Kalyani. He holds a gem-set bangle, a golden bow and a golden *kalasa,* a vase. It is believed that he will become a Buddha and many are the stories of how he will burn up the Bhuta Yakas—the hungry demons—and how he rides in a special chariot. Tissa knew that Nata Deva was honoured in Anuradhapura too. Later would this god be also identified as Avalokitesvara and Padmapani and statues would represent him holding a lotus bud. But that would be in later times when the aspect of the Bodhisat[177] would be accepted. Let it now suffice to know that in those early times the orthodox Buddhists of Lanka accepted no such. Later would the dilution occur and Nata would also be Ratnatilaka, the god of the golden brow adornment.

In the south, the god of Kataragama held special potency. This god had made his home in the fastness of the south-eastern jungles and had favoured the hero prince as he rode against the Damilas. His was the resplendent peacock throne even as he came out of Kadirapura holding his great Velayuda, his spear, protecting the oppressed. Around his neck does he wear the costliest gems and he carries a quoit, a chakra, and his hands reach out to grasp the moon. Only he, devotees say, can raise the flag of the devas, on which is emblazoned the figure of an Asura, and on his peacock vimana does he ride in great glory.

The people also acknowledged and honoured Siddha Pattini: she who burns up the demons, her right arm bearing the sacred bangle of her unearthly power. And oh, she is such a wonder-working guardian. Hadn't she turned the stone of Andungiri mountain to mud in which she grew paddy? Who else could reduce the black rock, the antimony of Andungiri to a rich mush? To this day we hear villages sing of her many states of divinity:

In water, musk, flower once born,
In rock, peak, cloth once born,
So the sixth, the seventh, in a mango born,
In such glory let supreme Pattini come.

In Sri Lanka's hill capital, Kandy, stand the temples of these guardians. It is obvious that Nata Deva is accepted as the avatar of Vibishana, brother of Ravana; and that Saman Deva, the god of Adam's Peak, was replaced by Kataragama Deva. Boksael gave way to Pattini. In his collection of *Sinhala Verse*, Nevil[178] has made some astute observations:

Boksael, a name of extreme obscurity and antiquity... referred to Pattini. There is a possibility of linking this, through the Chaldean Sala or Shala, goddess of war, with Pattini as Teda Pattini, and possibly Boksael or Boksal may be explained as connected with that name on one hand, and the Bodba or Vodva, the war goddess of the Celts, and the Bodilima, a hobgoblin spirit that terrified women and children in Ceylon with appalling cries on the other hand... In one tradition of Ceylon, Boksael is identified with Kalu Kumara, the black demon-prince, and it is possible that this represents the husband of the war goddess, whether Negal of Chaldea, not of Ireland or any other male form of the Sakti. In the later myths of Celtic lands there are obscure legends of a Black Knight who would answer well enough to a legendary form of Kalu Kumara.

How well indeed did the old-time Aryans take the goddesses to replace the gods!

Even as Tissa watched the unfolding of the ceremony, he was certain that with the inshore wind came a sweet tinkling sound. The smoke of burning incense turned pale red in the dawn sky and the sun, rising like a bright jewel, made the shadows blue, then silvery. The holy men were well pleased. Even as Vihara Maha Devi stepped to her palanquin, the chief priest of the Skanda temple held up a red homespun wrap. 'Wear it upon your knees as you travel, O queen,' he said, 'and this cloth of blue around your shoulders.'

Tissa told his mother, 'This is given that you remain in the care of the guardian gods, for see you, we have raised a *Mal Yahana*[179] on your behalf.'

As Vihara Maha Devi stepped into the litter, a small globe of light as bright as lightning hovered beside her and the tinkling of many bangles were heard. People prostrated themselves as the air took on the fragrance of flowers, the ripeness of mangoes.[180] The holy men raised their staffs, cried out their exhortations. Tissa nodded. Slowly, the riders moved out, the horse soldiers, the standard bearers, the criers. Men would bear the litter in teams; the royal attendants would follow the litter and a cohort of armed warriors walk their horses on either side. The grooms, servants, cooks and labourers travelled in ox carts behind the food wagons and at the rear, followed by a contingent of fighting men, came the heavy double-bullock wagon piled high with gifts. Vihara Maha Devi sighed. Dearly would she have wished to go with but a few. Indeed, she would have loved to simply walk the trails alone, but there was no help to it. She was queen of all Lanka, and as a queen would she have to go, even to satisfy her own whims.

The Enfolding Flower

LIFE BEGINS AS A BUD, OPENS SLOWLY WITH THE FRAGRANCE OF youth, flowers full, and, as the perianth weakens, each petal falls. Such a plant is life. It would put out its adventitious roots, its stems and tendrils, carry its own nectary, and in the full realization of its making, burst into bloom. This is the inflorescence of being, realizing, existing…and then the time of decay, the enfolding. Who would then think of the calyx once proudly held, that corolla of outer petals, those sepals of sensitivity, the stamens of determination and purpose? There comes a strange heaviness in the air and the weight of the years bends the stem.

There were tears in Vihara Maha Devi's eyes as the country curtsied to meet her. Yes, she would range as far as she would, even to the north-eastern harbour of Gonagama, but she was not, she told her escorts, on a journey. 'We go where we go as our spirit takes us. Is that understood?'

'But, O queen, have we no destination?'

'What is this you say? Must your every journey have a destination?'

The commander of the horse guard was bewildered. 'Then what road do we take, noble one?'

'Ah, you seek a road to somewhere. But this somewhere is where we say it will be. Is that hard to understand? See, now we desire to turn back awhile, take the road past the ford and skirt the hills. Our journey is not yours, good Mukund, so pay heed to our wishes. Also, do you prepare us a horse, for in the cool of the morning and evening will we ride and the litter may bear us when the day is hot.'

Mukund was puzzled. Where *was* the queen going? And she wished to ride. He thought of the bearers. 'We could let them ride in the carts and strap the litter to a wagon,' he told one of his men. 'Yes, that is what we can do, but I like this not. These trails are not as our coastal roads. The queen will tire herself much.'

Vihara Maha Devi smiled as she mounted. 'Now we will ride with you—that way.' The party turned, and the oxen made slight protest. 'To the great rock that guards the eastern forest. There will we go.' Turing to Mukund, she smiled broadly. 'Is that destination enough?'

They took the road to the Dastota ford. 'Are the carts strong enough for such a track?' she asked. 'I see no iron axles.'

'They are very strong, O queen, for our carpenters have found that the wood of a certain tree can be used that even serves the purpose of iron. This tree is found in many places in the south-east and it is called *Yakada Maran*. It is from this tree that the axles are fashioned.'

'That is good,' she said simply.

A moment later she said, 'The great rock calls to us and at its feet will we find shelter, for many caves of the holy men are to be found there.'[181]

This guardian rock is the highest point in the district of Tamankaduwa today—a district that holds some of Sri Lanka's most ancient ruins. One can see, from this point, the rock of Sigriya, the Veddah village of Horiwila and Egodapattu which is peopled even today by those of mixed Sinhalese and Tamil blood. From the peak one sees the ruins of Polonnaruwa and the Mahaweli river snaking its way through a sea of ruffled green. It is still wild country and the settlements of Yakkure, Horiwila and Dalukana are still threatened by bear and leopard.

'Know you that on our march to the holy city we fought the Damilas at the ford? The gods are ever with us. There, at the rock, do holy men stay. They will seek nothing from us, but we will ask of their blessing.'

Even as they approached the caves, fires were lit around the rock. Vihara Maha Devi sat at the feet of the mendicants who were but a few in number. 'Do the wild beasts trouble you?' she asked.

'They come and go, O queen. They know we do them no harm.'

'Yet will our men keep vigil.'

'It is well that the queen be so guarded.'

The months sped by. Riders whipped in and out, bringing Tissa the news of the queen's whereabouts, her health, her disposition. 'She is now at Oyagama,[182] lord.'

'There is no crossing there,' Tissa exclaimed. 'Does our mother wish to go to the other side?'

'No, lord, but she has bathed in the tank there, the Ranawarana Wewa. She tells us many tales of the Damila conquest. Commander Mukund bids me say that the queen seems to retrace the paths of the great campaign.'

Tissa relaxed. 'Then will she find herself in Anuradhapura before long. What route does she plan now?'

'She tells of the Kaluwara forest[183] and the place of the Chandrakanthi stones[184] lord.'

'But that is...that is far removed from where she now is!' He dismissed the rider and sat with troubled face. Was his mother grown so old that her mind wandered just as she was now doing? Surely this was an aimless journey. He smacked a palm on the hand-rest of his seat. He should never have permitted this journey. He summoned a guard. 'Bid the queen's courier to stay. Call the guards' captain.' To his chief commander he said, 'We ride out to escort the queen.'

'Do you accompany her to Anuradhapura, lord?'

'No. We return here. Prepare a state procession and the necessities of our visit to the holy city—gifts for the prince, much grain, and let each district bring gifts that we will take in their name. When we return with the queen will we travel with full regalia to the Rajarata.'

At the Ranawarana Wewa, Vihara Maha Devi, her hair diamond-splashed after her bath, told her women, 'Know you that in these waters did our son also bathe. Yes, for on his first return to Ruhuna did he come here with his champions and the generals of his army. The people called this the Ranveeru Ne Wewa, the tank where the heroes bathed. And here, where we now sit, did our son also sit and tell the people of the great victory. This was written down and called the Ranawarna Wewa Viththi—the account of the battle, the victory over the Damilas. All around this place are very ancient villages and tonight we will go to the parkland of Alutgoda where the temple of Peruwewa is, for there shall we rest.'

The birds called to them as they moved, quite leisurely, into the vast parkland. The whistles of the *Valpolkichcha*[185] filled the air and among the tall trees, Drunken Pipers[186] puffed their tails and hopped to and fro in a giddy dance of welcome.

The soldiers were wary. This was the typical haunt of the elephant, these ancient pathways of Ruhuna. Villagers had told them of the forays of lone raiders out of Wellawaya. The night in the small temple was speared by the sounds of the wilderness and there were the unmistakable snarls of leopard, the snuffle of bears and the throaty squeal of wild boar. At dawn, the howls of jackals roused many, and toque monkeys sat on the low walls.

'See,' said Vihara Maha Devi, 'even the anteater searches among the scrub. It is a beautiful day, is it not? We shall visit the sainted Theraputta in the aramya our son built for him. Surprised will he be, but I think not, for surely does he know of our coming.'

Mukund was pleased. Perhaps he could ask of the thera to exhort the queen to go back. He knew of the monk who had been one of Duttha Gamani's champions—a mighty man who, after the conquest, had sought to don the robe. Yes, he would not wish his queen to travel so.

They moved south-east, the parkland pocked with caves and rock outcrops and little rain pools and surrounded by lordly trees. The woods were dark, deep, and among the riot of *palu*,[187] satinwood, *milla*,[188] *mora*,[189] *kon*[190] and *mi*[191] stood the Deverum vihara where the mighty Theraputta Abhaya stood, hands raised in welcome.

'The queen still rides and asks no hand to help her dismount,' he said, 'yet she is tired and admits it not.'

Vihara Maha Devi was delighted to see the warrior–monk who had, as the villagers said, raised a huge stone slab, quite four-and-a-half-feet high and half that size in thickness in the centre of the Avasa, the stone-pitted shrine.[192] In the shrub rose a modest stupa, and the cells, the monastery, were of piled stone.

Carl Muller

'We see that our son has kept his promise, good thera. Did you need many men to build this vihara of stone?'

'Not many, for these arms are as strong as they were, and the work was easy.'

Mukund raised an eyebrow and muttered, 'Easy, he says. We will need elephants to move such rocks.'

The thera told of the tiny community. 'Some have come here from the outlying villages. The retreats are occupied, yet there is room for all. The forest creatures do not trouble us.'

'And where do the bricks come from?'

'The king sends great quantities. But come. Let the animals be watered and fed. There is ample water in the small lake yonder. The foresters have told us of your coming. They will wait with their women and sing for us tonight.'

It was an evening of such simple pleasure. The most charming songs were sung, and little girls, all chocolatey and big-eye, danced, and the women clacked sticks together as the men sang the songs of the soil. It was not long before the singing became a *tharangeta*[193] telling of the way the villagers relieved the tedium of their toil, whether in their *paelas*[194] or the *kamathas*.[195] It was a sturdy, large-voiced man who sang his challenge:

Hearken kind friends in that upper watch hut,
It is impossible to stop the wild pigs,
Let us sing loud! They will run away affrighted,
Let us sing the *sivpada*,[196] let us sing in competition.

It was a summons to the others to join in, and many weaved up to the fire to sing their stanzas.

Come, O sun, come and encircle us,
Come, O moon, come and encircle us.

Don't let the muddy water come into the clear stream,
Come all who would sing with me the sivpada.

Whereupon another would break in:

Until the sun god descends from the summit of the sun,
Until the moon god descends from the summit of the
moon,
Until *Gana Deviyo*[197] comes out of the abyss of the
darkness,
Sing we the sivpada as long as the *Irugala*[198] lasts.

Primitive, spontaneous music. So did the poor, the
unlettered, express themselves. 'Such a spirit of fellowship
is there in song,' Vihara Maha Devi murmured. 'Truly, we
hear no such in the palace.'

'This is the living heart of the land, O queen. It is song
that keeps the people firm of spirit. The young learn
from song; unhappiness is lost in song, grief is assuaged.
See now—they will sing their questions, sing the answers.
Unlettered they be, but unlearned they are not.'

Do you know what a sharp point is?
Do you know of what another sharp point is?
And do you know again of what a sharp point is?
And of yet another sharp point do you know?

The answer came smoothly:

One sharp point is the point for writing,
And there is the sharp point of the drill for boring,
A sharp point is that of the sewing needle,
And yet another is the sharp point of the cock's spur.

Another challenge was loudly voiced:

Do you know what a thalay[199] is?
And of another thalay do you know?
And do you know of one other thalay?
And of a thalay that is a name we know?

Carl Muller

Vihara Maha Devi laughed. 'Who would answer that? Why, there is the axe blade, the barber's blade, the warrior's blade, the blade of grass. Yet, he says thalay, which is a blade and surely not a blade of grass.'

Theraputta Abhaya's eyes twinkled. 'These forest dwellers are much versed. Listen to the first man for now he will make reply.'

The thalay is the blade that clears the jungle creepers,
The other is the e-thalay, the arrow that you shoot,
And there's the thalay which is the plain on which the cattle graze,
And there beyond the hills is Matale, surely another thalay!

They slept easily that night. The air was deliciously cool and the trees sighed and crooned and the leaves fell gently.

Tissa did not find his mother at the aramya of Theraputta Abhaya. He followed the trail: Buduruwayaya, the Amban Ganga, the tiny track near the cascade of Hiritiya Oya. 'Seven days,' he exclaimed, 'and she goes to the place of the ninety-seven caves. Where is that?'

The village headman could not say, but it was where a sapling of the holy tree of Anuradhapura had been planted.

'Sesuruwa!' Tissa exclaimed. 'The place of the bodhi rays. Is it there? No matter, it is on the north road. We will find it.'

It was two week later that Tissa met his mother on the pilgrim path. She sat beside a rock into which had been driven a metal trident. She showed no surprise at his coming. 'See, our son, is this not a marvel? The rock holds the trident, but who could have driven it in so? Many here worship the god Ganesh and strange tales do they tell of a holy man who made of these trees his shrine and drove his trident into the rock.'

Tissa shook his head. 'Long have we ridden to find you. Have you gone as far as Gonagama? And what is this place? It is desolate beyond belief.'

'Sanyasi Malai do the people call it. And see the small temple of the Buddha that stands on the plateau above us. One monk is there, and he is old and his sight fails him.'

Tissa listened amazed. The Wila Oya, the gleaming sweep of beaches and surf, the stops at the temples of Pillaiyar and Murugan, dust tracks, elephant trails... his mother had stopped at Kudumbigala, a wilderness of caves and scrub, salt flats, rice fields, the giant boulders of Yoda Lipa[200] and the deer plains of Bagura. 'Mother,' he said gently, 'it is time to return, for we must go to Anuradhapura.'

She nodded.

'We will turn back to the Kumbukkan Oya, where the shrine of Pattini is.'

She nodded.

'And on to Mahagalamuna and Magama. I will dispatch the carts, the bearers, much of the party on the long road back. We will take the shorter way.'

Her eyes seemed to smoulder. 'Think you we overdid our journey?'

'Nay, but it was not planned as we would have wished it to be, and you have wandered much, and time has passed swiftly.'

'Time!' she said and there was a hint of asperity in her voice. 'Think you that time is of such importance to us now? Time there is to return, to go to Rajarata, to lay our hands on the prince's head. That is all the time we need.'

They rode back, past the black Bowattagala rock and

the upthrust needles of Nelunpathpokunugala. Tissa was relieved when they reached Magama, relieved that his mother had begun to hum to herself when on the palace road. 'And what is that song you sing to yourself?' he smiled.

She turned in the saddle and her face was bright and the lines of tiredness seemed to have disappeared. 'Many songs did the forest people sing...Is all ready for our journey?'

'For many weeks has all been in readiness. But you must rest. Let us leave when you are well rested.'

She made no reply. When the festive meal was served that evening, Tissa bade an attendant carry invitation to the queen. Vihara Maha Devi did not appear.

'She sleeps, lord king. The lady of the chamber wishes that she be not disturbed.'

The palace stood in the south street and it was made known that all those who lived in the south and in the districts beyond the south moat would henceforth make their offerings, pay their taxes, to the prince Saliya and not to the king. The ministers listened to the complaints of the treasurer and questioned the wisdom of the royal decree. Did the king's government extend to the southern quarter or not? Would the people of the south care more for the prince and not the king? They made their objections known and Duttha Gamani found them in poor taste.

'And what would you say if we were to divide all we have into four parts and say, this one part is for the north, this other for the east, another for the south and the other for the west?'

'My lord, that would tell us that you give to each quarter what is needed, and so will the kingdom be developed.'

'Then what if we were to do the same for the city and its four quarters? Must we not develop the city too?'

'That must also be done, lord.'

'So see you then, what we give to the south comes to the city, does it not? Now do we wish that the south gives to the prince, and the prince in turn gives it back to the south. Is the understanding of such any difficulty, we ask.'

'No lord, yet who is to know how much will be so given and to what use it would be put...'

'Silence! Is it that you resent the prince? We see it plain that you do! What the prince does will the king know of.'

'What words are these!' he told his mother. 'It troubles us to hear our council speak in this way.'

'They only see what they see,' Vihara Maha Devi said. 'And soon they see two kings. That is what troubles them.'

'But why? Saliya will be our viceroy.'

'But a king surely. You give him all the privileges and trappings.'

'And that was your wish, mother. Or do you think we do too much?'

'You will never do too much. We will see your son and speak with him and he will mind what we say.'

There were two sets of ornaments. Prince Saliya needed to possess the insignia of royalty and a set of personal

Carl Muller

ornaments. There are many references to the five insignia of royalty and the sixty-four ornaments. Of these, the former needed to be carefully guarded, for they were treasure indeed. A king who lost his five insignia could well lose his kingdom, and any man who came into possession of the insignia could claim kingship. In the *Culavamsa* we are told of how the Damila king, Kulasekhara, when fighting the Sihala forces of Lankapura fled:

> ...he not only surrendered his courage, but also his throne, his ornaments and all else.

These times are yet to be written of, but we have cast ahead if only to illustrate how important the insignia are. In India, the five royal insignia were the *Rajakakudhabandhani,* and this is told of in the *Samkicca Jataka.*[201]

The *Saddharmaratnavaliya* names the insignia as the *mangul kaduwa,*[202] the *hela kudaya,*[203] the *nalal pata,*[204] the *val viduna*[205] and the *ran mirivadi sangala.*[206]

To these are added the *chatta*[207] and the *ekavali.*[208]

Saliya was a vision of silver. No gold did he wear. Even his personal ornaments—bracelet, armlet, rings, bangles, robe, calf bangles, earrings, slippers, girdle, waist chain, scarf and turban were of silver. The ceremony was conducted with all necessary ritual and great care was taken that the silver turban was wound round the prince's head, then tied behind, the ends drawn over the shoulders to be tucked into the waistband. The sprinkling was done by the holy men, the ministers and merchants of the city. Saliya then occupied the fig-wood seat and received the silver insignia. As required, he next left his seat to approach the heavy gold-draped chairs in which sat Duttha Gamani, the queen and his uncle Tissa. The chamber was hushed as he received their blessing and Duttha Gamani rose to lead him back to his seat. 'King are you, our son, for king will you be, and now do you perform as a king under our kingship. Listen now to the wise ones who will tell you of the dignity of a yuvaraja.'[209]

Vihara Maha Devi settled back in her chair as the chaplain explained, in an emotionless voice, that the dignity of the yuvaraja lay in a position of trust. 'It carries rights, and a share in the great work of governance, O prince, and it is the pleasure of the great monarch Duttha Gamani Abhaya, thy father, that you will henceforth support his royal office. This title has our lord of the land conferred on you, and all that is given unto you is that you be truly and wholly contented. Thus are you also *mahadipada*[210] for it is sought that you would be, above all else, true king... and thus do you henceforth enjoy the regal dignities of governor and sub-king and accordingly have you received the sacred unction; and in the wearing of the *usnisa*[211] assume sovereignty over the southern quarter of the city and the southern districts thereof, for you are held proficient in the science of arms, in religion and in all the arts and sciences that are the necessities for regal succession. Now do I in role as chaplain, and as personal adviser to the lord of Lanka in all matters, be they spiritual, temporal, official or private...now do I ask before all assembled here: this noble company, the Maha Sangha, the court and the people...now do we say to thee, be thou king of the southern quarter and, in the fullness of time, king of all the land.'

Saliya looked at his father, the queen, the ranks of monks. All he had to do was to accept. His eyes strayed over the throng, the people, warriors, merchants. Where were they of the low caste? But he knew that in that east-road village of the chandala, flags would be raised—silver flags for a silver king. He said to the chaplain: 'I will be king of the southern quarter and southern districts.'

Vihara Maha Devi sighed. It was over, and suddenly she did not wish to attend the revels that would follow. A week of festivity had been ordered and there would be a week-long alms-giving to the Sangha. Thousands of monks from many parts of the country had come to the city and there would be all-night chanting before the *paritta*[212] was tied on the prince's wrist. For Vihara Maha Devi, it was all too much. The smoke of the braziers hurt her eyes and the echo of the drums made her press her knuckles into her temples. 'We will go to the wewa,' she said.

'The wewa? But it grows dark and there will be no moon for another hour,' Duttha Gamani said.

'Yet will we go, for my head throbs and the evening air will be soothing. An attendant will we take. There will we sit and see the lights of Mihintale on the far shore and the spirits of the dusk will sing to us.'

Tissa told his brother, 'Our mother will have her way. Much worry did she cause us when she went around the country.'

'And that should you have prevented. She is not fit enough to undertake such hazardous journeys.'

Tissa nodded and took his brother's hand. 'We couldn't hold her back, and can you hold her back now? Can you command her to stay? No brother. She will go to the wewa as she wishes and neither you nor I can prevent her doing so.'

'We like it not. Hush, she comes.'

Vihara Maha Devi looked at her sons. 'So stern of countenance, the two of you. Do you disagree as of old or do you now join forces to disagree with me?'

'Mother, it is late—and you...you...'

'Yes, say it. I am old and now we must mind our years and become but shadows of ourselves and seek not anything but the end of being old. And that is the end we all reach.' She held them close to her and her fingers tightened as if she wished to be part of them. 'My sons,' she said, 'my dream is you and both of you have followed this dream and this is now our land and we are one people and there is peace. The years of death are over. And even as you followed our dream, we followed you. Your happiness was ours, as your triumphs and conquests. You, Tissa, have you not made of Ruhuna a resplendent country…and you, our disobedient one, have we not been a part of your greatness? Know you now how a mother loves and think you, have we had the time to love ourselves? Our land…and you, Tissa, wished us not to journey forth to look on it…'

'But mother, we feared for you!'

'That we knew, but why fear for me? Fear rather for this land. Guard it, protect it, hold it close and fear for all in it. And do you also fear that we go to the wewa now? Why? Will the crocodiles come upon us or will assassins wait for us on the path?'

'Mother, you jest. If to the wewa you must go, we will walk with you.'

'No. There is the ritual of the thread and the alms to the monks. Do not ignore your duty as a king.'

'Then Tissa shall go with you.'

'Tissa too must remain. Does he not represent the southern kingdom. Are you both unmindful of your duties?'

'But remain with us tonight. You can go to the wewa in the light of day.'

'We will go now! The moon will soon rise, and the wavelets will move like silver leaves, and there, against the night clouds rises the hill of Mahinda and even these old eyes can see the tiny lights of the monks in their temple on the plain of the mango tree. And know you, our sons, wherever we go and whatever the journey, a mother's love remains with you forever.'

'That we know full well. Must you go?'

'We must…and an attendant will we take. Come, embrace us, our sons, and do not look so troubled.'

'It is as if she bids us farewell,' said Tissa morosely. 'Do you see who goes with her?'

'Her chamber woman, Kumuda.'

'Well, she has gone as she said she would. Nothing can make her change her mind.'

Saliya came up. 'The queen bid me farewell with much intensity of feeling. Is it that she goes on a journey, father?'

'Only to the wewa. Why, what did she say?'

'She gave us her love. She stroked my face. Father, her rings are so loose on her fingers.'

'Eh? What?'

Tissa laughed shortly. 'When one grows old, rings grow loose on fingers that shrink. Know you how old your grandmother is?'

Saliya shook his head. 'She touched my face. Never have I known her do so before.'

'She is, above all, a mother,' said Duttha Gamani, 'and no mother has loved so.'

The red road to the bund of the Tissa Wewa lay like a long weal scabbing an angry black under the bunching *wewarani* trees.[213] The evening thickened and Vihara Maha Devi, looking down from the soft sand of the bund, saw the city, light-spattered, the Morse-coding of rushlights as men and women walked homewards. Kumuda, a lean woman in her forties, heard the splash of water and the distinct slap of the tails of crocodiles as they fed.

'My lady...see, white balls like lime. There, near those rocks. The droppings of the crocodiles. And I hear them in the water...we must go back.'

'We need not fear them. They will not trouble us.'

Kumuda, like many women of the villages, had many strange ideas about the reptiles. She was certain that they had four eyes and that their bites caused leprosy. Why, even the elephant and the buffalo were wary of these creatures... and those white balls, so like lime. The creatures surely crawled the bund at night.

'We will sit here, Kumuda. It is a good place, among these rocks. There, yonder, is the bodhi *maeda*[214] and see that open ground now cleared and made ready for the Maha Thupa. It is said that throughout this *kalpa*[215] will the holy tree diffuse the Buddha rays and remove all evil.' They sat, and Vihara Maha Devi sighed. 'Last night did we dream of an altar of offerings, and when we approached, the awning opened. Strange it was that we saw ourself no more when we passed through, and yet, such peace of mind was there when we awoke.'

'It seems to grow even darker, my lady. Why do we remain here?'

'It was the voice of our waking hour. We wait that we find ourself beyond the awning of our dream. That is what the voice promised.'

Kumuda leaped to her feet as a sleek creature scurried by, red eyes glinting fiercely. It gave a rasping screech and disappeared in the shadows. 'A, a mongoose...it hunts the serpent. We must be away, O queen, we must...'

'Hush woman. Know you the story of the mongoose? In the south do the people of the settlements beside the

Carl Muller

tanks sing of the poor woman of Sravasti who kept a tame mongoose. Know you the tale?'

'Quiet. Listen, is that not the sound of crocodiles that feed in the water?

Kumuda looked around wildly, gave a cry. Far in the blackness, the mountain of Mahinda shone like a silvered cone and in the water a strange vessel moved: a barge covered all around with an aura of electric blue, gleaming from stem to stern. On the deck stood many forms, dark, silhouetted against the blue clasp of the light. At the stem stood three forms, taller, statelier and from their gold headbands issued lances of light that flared on the water, dissolving in myriad swirls of umber and white.

'My queen, m-my queen, what is it—what...what are they...my queen...' The woman's voice broke from a coarse, frightened whisper to a wailing shriek. Vihara Maha Devi had slipped to the ground, lay there cocooned in her cloak, her face so white that every dark hair that stirred against her cheeks in the breeze could be counted. From the barge came a cry that shivered the air and all around rose voices of lamentation. Even the wind sobbed.

Kumuda crouched, her head hidden in her arms, her body heaving. She felt the press of a hand on her shoulder and fearfully raised her head, saw the dark women stand around the queen, wring their hands and wail thinly. A woman in a starry robe, her face soft, illumined, motioned to her to rise. 'Come O companion of her last hour. We are but wraiths and shadows of the regions of bliss. Help us you must. Rise, be not afraid.'

Kumuda looked around wildly. Could she break free, run? What would these creatures do? Had they killed the queen. She gave a despairing cry. 'Who, who are you...

don't hurt me...don't...the queen...what has happened to her? What...'

The hand on her shoulder was soothing. Suddenly, she felt assured. 'The queen but sleeps, and now does she dream and knows what lies beyond the awning of the altar of offerings. Come, faithful servant, you must lay her in the barge.'

'But, but where do you take her?'

'To life. Life new and glorious. Life beyond all pain and care.'

'Do you...do you take me too?'

'Do you then seek to die?'

Kumuda's mind reeled. 'The queen...the queen is dead!' She screamed, then fell beside the prostrate form, fingers fumbling to draw away the cloak. Again, soft hands touched her, again the feather-brush of divine compassion.

'Place her in the barge. We take her to where she will live on. See how yonder mountain glows. There do the devas await her.'

How light she was. Kumuda rose, her queen in her arms and no weight did she feel. The water lay still around the vessel and on the deck sat three women with golden bands around their foreheads. They nodded and one spread her arms, laid the queen's head on her lap and wept. Beads of crystal fell on the white, bloodless face, and as Kumuda stared, the eyes opened and a soft fire seemed to burn in them. The voice was at her ear. 'We go now, Kumuda, and you will return to our sons and tell them of our passing.'

'My queen—you live! But what will become of me? Surely will I be slain. What shall I say to the king...where will I go. Will I not be put to death for abandoning you?'

Carl Muller

'Nay, good Kumuda, for the devas will give to our sons the sign of our passing. Fear not, and do you give to our sons this word: Say to them that we are among the shining ones...say to them that there will we remain, but when this land has need of us, we will return. Let their voices be raised as a fountain to us, both day and night, and let no shrine be raised, for we do not die but lie in the long sleep of our reward. We go to the holy mountain. Go ye now, and keep us ever in your mind.'

The moon rose in a flood of silver and the road sparkled, and every pebble was a knowing eye.

Kumudu watched the barge slowly move away, following the path of moonlight and tottered back as a great light filled the sky over Mihintale. She stood alone, and turning stumbled away.

> ...and the barge with oar and sail
> Moved from the brink, like some full-breasted swan
> That, fluting a wild carol ere her death,
> Ruffles her pure cold plume, and takes the flood
> With swarthy webs...[216]

'Our mother is dead,' Duttha Gamani said. 'We will give to the woman Kumuda a fine dwelling and land in the northern quarter where she may remain.'

Tissa looked bleakly at the rising bund of the wewa. 'She came to us, brother, as we lay asleep...just as she came to you. Alms must we give to the brotherhood, and she bids us remain here, build with thee the great thupa.'

'Aye, that must we now do, for the waiting time is almost over. She waited with us...and now when the work must begin, she left us.' Duttha Gamani clutched at his head. 'We have lost so much. More than all this life can say. Surely is all the land in mourning.'

'From coast to coast, brother. The monks have sheathed the tongues of the bells and soft do they peal, on and on and on.'

Everywhere in the land, the trees shed their flowers. The roads, the car tracks, the hillsides, the rolling slopes, lay cloaked with the falling chalices of butter-yellow allamanda, white cape jasmines, bright pink crepe myrtle, red oleander and purple sanderiana. Pink wax flowers and yellow arbour vine fell lazily, and creamy-white bridal bouquets starred the grass as did the large-headed candytufts.

The flowers seemed to know that the island's most precious flower was no more.

Endnotes

Silver

1. This cave is about eight *yojana*s south of Anuradhapura. In *Ancient Inscriptions in Ceylon*, E.Muller identifies it as the cave within which the ancient Rajatalena Vihara was built, known as the Ridi Vihara today. Rhys Davids said that the distance between Anuradhapura and the cave was 55 miles as the crow flies. Legend has it that the temple was built within the cave in the latter times of Duttha Gamani.

2. This practice of giving respect and honour to that group of supernatural beings called sylvan deities was prevalent. Such wood spirits or *vana muru* continued to be worshipped and, as the *Muvadev-da-Vata* says, it was a long-established tradition. In the *Saddharmaratnavaliya* there is mention of a spirit that resided in a *midella* [*Barringtonia*] tree and of another god in a *timbiri* tree [*Diospyros embryopteris*] who gave a holy thera divine food. Even the Bo tree was considered the repository of a deity, and this is mentioned in the *Attanagaluvamsaya*.

3. A port on the east coast, near the mouth of the Kala Oya, about 40 miles from Anuradhapura.

4. The *Rajavaliya* confirms that a certain forest tree gives relief to leprosy patients, and that food prepared from the bark is an effective cure.

5. Seven yojanas north of Anuradhapura, a little over 50 miles.

6 Parker gives us details of the small earth-bund tank in *Ancient Ceylon*. The tank is now called Vavuni Kulam.

7. Forest hermit.

8. Mihantale.

9. Adam's Peak.

10. Modern Rambodagalla, in the highlands of Ambatthakola.

Ratnavalli

11. Forbes: *Eleven Years in Ceylon*, 1841.

12. *Anu*—ninety; *raja*—king; *pura*—city.

13. Attributed to Parakrama Pandya Arikesari Deva.

14. Called the Basavak Kulam today.

15. Scavengers.

16. As told in *Children of the Lion*.

17. Sinhala: *Hatareskotuwa*.

18. Pinnacle.

19. This is told of in the *Anagatavamsa*—Pundit Wattadara Medhananda Thera, 1960.

20. *Rajavaliya*, pp. 1–4.

21. This is specified in the *Nikaya Sangrahaya*—Weeragoda Amaramoli Thera, 1934.

22. As given in the *Rajavaliya*.

23. In *Kuveni Asna*—Kiriella Gnanawimala Thera, 1957.

24. In his *Kavyasekharaya*—Canto XI verse 17, Canto X verses 103 and 146, 1957.

25. In *Jatika Pota* by Naulle Dhammananda and Devinuwara Ratnajoti Theras, 1955 (a telling of the *Kusanali Jataka*).

26. March/April.

27. S.G. Vasu: *Daily Practice of the Hindus.*

28. In the *Mayamataya*, the rishis say that a tree that is thin at the top is female; one that is thin in the middle is sexless; one of uniform thickness is male. If thin at the top, it is the home of a fierce she-demon. If it has a drum-like trunk,

it can be cut without fear. A hollow tree, if felled, brings much sorrow.

29. Also *Hal-gaha—Vateria acuminata.*
30. *Bassia longifolia.*
31. The dwellings of priests.
32. Lion thrones.
33. Royal palaces.
34. Dimunitive, short, tiny maiden.
35. The account of this is given in Chapter 9—'Brother against Brother'—in *Children of the Lion.* Forced to flee with his men into the hills, Duttha Gamani went to the Kotmalaya region where he remained until his father's death.
36. The account of this is found in Chapter 41—'The Amethyst Wine'—in *Children of the Lion.*
37. In north India. Also called Udenipura.
38. The Buddha—the sage of the Sakya clan.
39. The arahat Mahinda, son of Emperor Asoka came to the mountain of Mihintale to preach the doctrine of the Buddha. It has long been credited that this was the beginning of the way of the Buddha in Lanka, but this is contradicted by the story of the Buddha's three visits to the island in earlier times where, as the *Mahavamsa* says, thousands embraced the faith and set their feet on the Buddhist path. The writer also draws attention to a recent lecture on *The Pre-History and Early History of Sri Lanka* delivered at the Colombo University by the late Dr S.U. Deraniyagala, archaeological commissioner, where he disclosed details of earlier settlers who migrated to Lanka during prehistoric and early historical times. He showed how over 7,000 years ago, a large portion of India and Sri Lanka was a single landmass and that the human groups that would have inhabited this in earlier periods, would have had the same, or been similar in characteristics to each other in genetic structure and cultural heritage. He said that the first writing in Lanka appeared on potsherds from Anuradhapura, dated to 600 BC and in Brahmi script,

and is certain evidence of writing in Lanka even before the arrival of Vijaya and the arahat Mahinda. He emphasized that there was an established civilization, urbanization, and that Buddhism was known in those times. It is also significant to note that the remains of glazed alms bowls, as used in north India in the time of the Buddha, have been unearthed in Anuradhapura, belong to a period 300 years before the arrival of Mahinda.

40. Oliver Weerasinghe, 'City that Influenced Buddhist History', in *Viskam—Creativity*, a souvenir on the occasion of the 5th Non-Aligned Summit Conference, Sri Lanka, 9–20 August, 1976.

Towering Faith

41. W. Geiger, *Dipavamsa and Mahavamsa*, Leipzig, 1905.
42. C.P. Malalasekera, *The Pali Literature of Ceylon*.
43. Sacred verses.
44. The Buddhist canonical law.
45. These are the five groups of sacred verses.
46. *Dipavamsa*, ed. and tr. Oldenberg, 1879.
47. B.C. Law, *On the Chronicles of Ceylon*, Delhi.
48. G.P. Malalasekera, *Pali Lierature in Ceylon*.
49. 'Rain—When and Where We Want It'—Article in the *Island*, national newspaper of Sri Lanka, 27 June 1995.
50. In Sri Lanka to this day, gokkola is used in the construction of *poruwa*s (the platforms upon which bride and grooms stand at their wedding ceremonies); *pirit mandapa*s (cubicles within which monks chant the sacred slokas); and woven into elaborate constructions such as *torana* (ceremonial arches) and other structures.
51. According to tradition, butter clay is the best clay of all, always retaining its moistness.
52. All worldly pleasures.

Endnotes

53. Indus.

54. Such invocation to the seven sacred rivers is still uttered by Buddhists of Sri Lanka and the Hindus of Bengal—a sense of affinity that brings close, in a geographic sense, the pervasion of a culture that embraces both peoples.

55. This ancient monastery was built by king Kavantissa. The ruins are believed to lie in modern Badagiriya, about seven miles north of Hambantota on the southern coast.

56. Benares.

57. Situated at the confluence of Varna and Asi, tributaries of the Ganges, 80 miles below Allahabad on the north bank of the Ganges. Benares obviously derived its name from these two tributaries.

58. *Buddhavamsa,* ed. R. Morris, Pali Text Society, 1882.

59. *Majjhima Nikaya,* Volumes I–IV, eds V. Trenckner, R. Chalmers and Ms Rhys Davids, Pali Text Society, 1888–1925.

60. *Diyavadana,* eds E.B. Cowell and R.A.Neil, Cambridge, 1886.

61. The Maitreya or Meteyya Buddha.

62. Universal monarch.

63. This prophecy of the future of Benares is found in *Digha Nikaya,* Volume I–III, eds T.W. Rhys Davids, J.E. Carpenter and W. Stede, Pali Text Society, 1890–1911.

64. The mental processes.

65. Buddhists acknowledge six inner or personal bases as Ajjhatika and a corresponding six external bases as Bahira. The first is the physical sense organs and the mind base or consciousness. The other six are sense objects, and together they form the beginning of the process of cognition upon which the mental processes depend. While it may not be that the king wished to give the thupa a 'mind' it is a fact that the thupa rose on twelve layers of material.

66. In Sinhala: 'Enough brother.'

67. This historic cetiya lies about two kilometres from Buttala town, close to the spot where Tissa built yet another dagaba about six miles from the Dematamal vihara. Today, one

travels about 230 km from Colombo to reach these ancient dagabas. Archaeological excavations have confirmed the existence of a shrine as well, which had fallen into ruin.

68. This great struggle is detailed in Chapter 9 of *Children of the Lion*: 'The Triumph of Pandukabhaya'.

69. After Panduk Abhaya became king, he gave Ritigala to the Sangha. Duttha Gamani also returned the mountain and all its buildings to the monks. It was only in 1995 that archaeologists began to restore the ruins that were encrusted with many layers of mud. An ayurvedic centre has also been brought to light and a number of caves around the slopes contain broken granite statues of the Buddha and many rock inscriptions.

70. This was a small vihara situated to the west of the Brazen Palace, where monks who chanted the Suttas remained. Ref. *Digha Nikaya Atthakatha—Sumangalavilasini,* Volumes I–III, eds T.W. Rhys Davids, J.E. Carpenter and W. Stede, Pali Text Society, 1886–1932.

71. Recitals.

72. *Dhammapada Atthakatha,* I–IV. ed., H. Smith, H.C. Norman and L.S. Tailang, Pali Text Society, 1906–1915. Reference is made to dighabanaka Dhammapada Banaka Maha Tissa thera, who lived in the time of Duttha Gamani.

73. Ruby or cinnabar.

74. This Bhanika system was in practice in ancient times because writing, although known, was little used. In India also this was a way of preserving ancient Vedic literature. In Buddhism, the origin of the bhanikas may be traced to the tradition where certain elders were made responsible for the preservation of sections of the Buddhist canon. The *Vinya* was entrusted to Upali, the *Digha Nikaya* to Ananda, the *Majhima Nikaya* to the disciples of Sariputta, the *Samyutta Nikaya* to Maha Kasappa and the *Anguttara Nikaya* to Anuruddha. This is told of in the *Samantapasadika* and the *Mahabodhivamsa.* It must be also noted that in later times, there were the

Suttantikas who were versed in the Suttas, the Vinyadharas who were expert in the Vinya, and the Matikkhadharas or Abhidhammikas, the masters of the doctrine (*Vinyapitaka*, Volumes I–IV, ed. H. Oldenberg, London 1879–83). The dighabanakas were the reciters of the Digha Nikaya, the Majjhimabhanikas the reciters of the Majjhima Nikaya. There is little doubt that the bhanika system first crystallized in India and was then introduced to Lanka. In the *Milindapanha* (ed. V. Trenckner, Pali Text Society, 1962) we are told how the Suttantikas were the masters of the Suttas; a Vinyika the master of the Vinya; the Abhidhammika the master of the doctrine and a Dhammakathika an expounder of the doctrine, a Jatakabhanika a master of the Jatakas, &c. There is also epigraphical evidence of bhanikas in India, especially among the famous Bharut monuments (Baru and Sinha, *Bharut Inscriptions*). Several texts tell of these reciters. Among them are the *Patancasudani*, *Atthasalini*, *Manorathapurani*, *Samantapasadika*, *Maduratthavilasini*, *Paramatthajotika II*, *Sammohavinodani*, *Visuddhajanavilasini* and the *Mahavamsa,* to name a few. Unfortunately, there began to develop different schools of opinion and divergent views that eventually caused divisions in the community of monks.

75. In Rhys Davids' *Dialogues of the Buddha* as well as in the Pali Text Society edition of the *Sumangalavilasini*, and in the *Thupavamsa*, we are told that the corporeal relics that remained of the Buddha after cremation at Kusinara, were divided into eight shares and given to the representatives of eight cities. However, seven of these shares were miraculously removed from under the stupas built over them and conveyed to Rajagraha, where king Ajatasatru deposited them in a subterranean chamber, intending that they come into the hands of Emperor Asoka who would distribute the relics all over the world. The remaining share, enshrined at Ramagrama, passed into the hands of the Naga kings of the underworld and then found their way to the Maha Thupa in Anuradhapura.

76. A class of demigods that indulge in heavenly bliss and terrestrial pleasures. They inhabit the lower regions of the firmament and remain over the tops of large trees, and sport in forests, streams and on hills.

77. The white water lily is one of the five kinds of lotus and is called helmeli. The others are ambula, upula, rathpiyum and helapiyum—the purple water lily, blue lotus, red lotus and white lotus.

78. Tr. C.D.R. Bastian Jayaveera Bandara, Colombo, 1926.

79. Kenneth H. Myers, *Success Through Quartz Crystals,* Metro Manila, Philippines, 1989.

80. The Woodapple tree—*Feronia elephantum.*

81. The drinking coconut or young king coconut.

Saliya

82. This period covers the rise and fall of Rome, the Byzantine era and through the Dark Ages to the Middle Ages.

83. George Wall, *Introduction to a History of the Industries of Ceylon* and 'Industries of Ceylon', *Journal of the Royal Asiatic Society,* Ceylon Branch, Vol. X, 1888.

84. Ibid.

85. Ibid.

86. Pura Deva was a god who presided over Anuradhapura and whose shrine existed in the times before Duttha Gamani. This shrine fell into neglect and became a derelict.

87. This merit book or *punna pothaka* held a record of all the meritorious deeds of a person. This was then read out at the person's death bed, thus gladdening the mind and heart of the dying man, purifying his thoughts and ensuring a happy rebirth. It may seem that all the religion practised by the kings were limited to such deeds of merit, and they were desirous of acquiring merit of as many kinds as possible. The *Papancasudani,* which is the Commentary on the *Majjhima Nikaya* (ed. Siri Dhammarama, Colombo, 1917 and 1926)

also mentions that monks kept a notebook or *mutthi pothaka* in which they wrote of the virtues of the Buddha and the Dhamma.

88. Secretary.

89. Some scholars believe that these elephant carvings and delicate bas reliefs relate to the south Indian art of the Pallava period of the seventh century. While confessing to some liberties, the writer reminds that the same sculptor could have also carved the elephants in the royal pleasure gardens at Anuradhapura.

90. The eight nidhis are said to be the divine treasures of the god of riches, Kuvera. Their nature is not exactly defined although some appear to be equated with precious stones. The nidhis are Padma, Mahapadma, Sanka, Makara, Kachchapa, Mukunda, Nanda, Nila and Kharba. In the tantric system, these nidhis are personified and accepted as demigods who are attendant on Kuvera or Lakshmi.

91. This has since been rendered into Sinhalese and edited by A.P. Buddhadatta, 1959. It is also referred to as the *Sahassavatthuppa-karana*.

92. These are found on pp. 451–2 and p. 607.

93. Also Rattamalakanda, five miles south of Anuradhapura and known as Ratmale today.

94. A ceremonial archway over the stairs. The original design does not exist today. Both stairway and platform have been rebuilt.

95. *Ceylon: An Account of the Island—Physical, Historical and Topographical*, London, 1859.

96. In translation by John M. Seneviratne of Sylvain Levi, 'Chino-Sihalese Relations in the Early and Medieval Ages', *Journal of the Royal Asiatic Society*, Ceylon Branch, Vol. XXIV, 1915–16; and Seneviratne, 'Some Notes on Chinese References', in the same journal.

97. Ed. R.S. Pandit, Allahabad, 1935.

98. Cloth of Sihala.

99. Also ref. *Artibus Asiae,* Vol. XXIV, 1962, and C.Notton, *Histoire du Dhammaraja et Noite Signeur,* Vol. I, Paris, 1926.

100. *Natural History,* ed. and tr. H. Rackham, Harvard, 1942.

101. Canopus is one of the twenty-two brightest stars with an absolute magnitude of minus 4.6 and it is 200 light years from Earth.

102. Tr. Pandit Bapu Deva Sastri, Calcutta, 1861.

103. A religious school.

104. Over 2,000 years have passed and to this day there is no evidence of any decay in this foundation and no part of the superstructure has given way because of any fault of the base.

105. This is told of in Chapter 37, *Children of the Lion,* 'The Reinforcing of Ruhuna'.

106. This title is borne by the heir apparent and when given, the bearer usually succeeds as paramount king. Such title had to be formally conferred by the reigning monarch.

107. Kelaniya today.

108. President of the council.

109. The House of secretaries or scribes.

110. The officer in charge of the administration of the city and its environs.

111. The long white, sweet-smelling flowers of the Indian Cork Tree.

112. The traditional constituents of the army: elephant corps, cavalry, chariots and infantry.

113. Commander of the army.

114. Also called Ho. In Pali and Sanskrit, it is Asoka (*Jonesia asoka*).

The Chandala Maid

115. Viscount George Valentia, *Voyages and Travels to India, Ceylon, the Red Sea, Abyssinia and Egypt in the Wars 1802, 1803, 1804, 1805 and 1806,* London, 1809.

116. The Pali (or Pally) were the washers for low castes; the Kinnara were mat weavers; and the Rodi the eaters of dead animals and makers of elephant nooses. These were the despised and degraded castes.

117. R.W. Ievers, *Manual of the North Central Province, Ceylon*, Colombo, 1899.

118. Robert Knox, *An Historical Relation of the Island of Ceylon in the East Indies*, Royal Society, 1681.

119. Bryce Ryan, *Caste in Modern Ceylon*, New Delhi, 1993.

120. This is 'Hamuduruwane' or 'Hamuduru' today, which means nobleman, leader of a clan, religious dignitary, head of a family, etc. The word is shortened to 'Hamu' in many cases, but said in full in the case of a monk or religious leader.

121. Probably 'Mudiyanse'—a term used today especially for one who has excelled in his particular calling.

122. Arrack—the alcoholic brew made from the toddy of the coconut palm.

123. 'Appu' today.

124. Could be 'Adigah' which is an honorific.

125. Joao Ribeiro, *History of Ceylon*, tr. P.E. Pieris, Galle, Sri Lanka.

126. Jaggery makers.

127. Tributes, designated quantities, duties as in customs duties.

128. Quantity of work or earnings thereof.

129. This refers to the five eyes a person of great saintliness possesses. They are the bodily eye (*mamsacakkhu*), the heavenly eye (*dibba*) by which he sees everything that comes to pass in the universe, the eye of understanding (knowledge); the eye of omniscience, and the Buddha eye by means of which he beholds the saving truth. A saint is also said to be possessed of any or all of the *chalabhinna*—the six supranormal powers. The six *abhinna* are the power of *iddhi* (flight), the heavenly ear which is the supranormal power of hearing, the power to read the thoughts of others, the knowledge of former

existences, the heavenly eye which is the supranorml power of seeing, and the abandonment of the asavas or desires. (Rhys Davids, *Dialogues of the Buddha*, and Aung; *Compendium of Philosophy*.) Arahats are also endowed with the four special sciences (*Patisambhida*)—a transcendent faculty in grasping the meaning of a text or subject; the ability to grasp the law of all things as taught by the Buddha; to know the meaning of all things in exegesis, and a readiness in expounding and discussion.

Sumanavo

130. A mountain on the eastern part of the kingdom of Anuradhapura.

131. The elephant does extend its hind legs backwards as a man does when he kneels, instead of bringing them under his body like any other four-footed creature. Prior to the seventeenth century, Europeans believed that the elephant had no joints and could not lie down to rest but had to sleep standing, leaning its bulk against a tree. In 1633, John Donne gave us these lines that readers will find in his *Progress of the Soul:*

Nature's great masterpiece, an Elephant,
The only harmless great thing
Yet Nature hath given him no knee to bend;
Himself he up-props, on him relies...

Shakespeare was also misinformed. In *Troilus and Cressida* we read:

The elephant hath joints, but none for courtesy;
His legs are for necessity, not flexure.

132. Dr Granville Dharmawardene, Scientific paper presented at the 52nd Annual Sessions of the Sri Lanka Association for the Advancement of Science, November 1996. From this paper, an article titled, 'Reincarnation: Now a Scientifically

Acceptable Phenomenon' was featured in the *Ceylon Daily News* on 7 August 1997.

133. In *Children of the Lion,* Chapter 32, 'On Her Majesty's Service'.

134. *Humboldtia laurifolia.* The flowers of this shrub grow in clutches of eight or ten, and attract ants.

135. *Hoya carnosa.* A creeper that thrives on the trunks of trees.

136. Also known as the Pudding Pipe tree; *ehala* in Sinhala and *tirukontotai* in Tamil. This tree is common in the dry regions of Sri Lanka and India. In season, the flowers are taken for temple offerings, while the astringent bark is used for tanning and for the preparation of native medicines.

137. Literally, son of god. A deity.

138. The palace of enlightment.

139. The *Lalitavistara,* found in the *Buddhist Hybrid Sanskrit Grammar and Dictionary* (ed. F. Edgerton, Yale, 1953) tells of the guardians of the Bodhi Mandala. The account of the coming of the bodhi tree to Lanka is told of in *Children of the Lion,* Chapter 23, 'Samgamitta'.

140. The helm of a ship.

141. The *Mahavamsa Atthakatha* (ed. G.P. Malalasekera, Pali Text Society, 1925–7) calls the nunnery Sirivaddhagara. In *Encyclopaedia of Buddhism,* Vol. II, 1966, H.R. Perera records that the nuns of the Upasika vihara later came to be known as Hatthalhaka bhikkunis and continued to be called so even after other sects arose.

142. This title was conferred upon Maha Arittha.

143. A recital of the faith.

144. This is also told of in the *Vinaya Atthakatha,* Volumes I–VII, eds. Takakusa and M. Nagai, Pali Text Society, 1924–47).

145. M.B. Ariyapala: *Society in Medieval Ceylon,* Colombo, 1956.

146. J.J. Meyer, *Sexual Life in Ancient India,* Vols. I and II, London, 1930.

147. Tr. Chandra Rajan, Penguin India, 1993.

148. Ed. Gnanesvara Nayaka Thera, Colombo, 1914.

149. Ed. D.B. Jayatilake, Colombo, 1936.
150. Ed. M. Siddhartha Thera, Colombo, 1926.
151. Ed. B. Saddhatissa Thero, Panadura, Ceylon.

A Question Of Succession

152. This is further explained in the introduction in *Children of the Lion*.
153. M.B. Ariyapala, *Society in Medieval Ceylon*, Colombo, 1956.
154. N.N. Law, *Aspects of Ancient Indian Polity*, Oxford, 1921.
155. Ed. D.B. Jayatilake, Colombo, 1936.
156. Ed. Nanesvara Nayake Thera, Colombo, 1914.
157. R. Mehta, *Pre-Buddhist India*, Bombay, 1939.
158. Miss P.C. Dharma, *The Ramayana Polity*, Madras, 1941.
159. H.W. Codrington, *A Short History of Ceylon*, London, 1926.
160. F.A. Hayley, *A Treatise on the Law and Customs of the Sinhalese*, Colombo, 1923.
161. *Srimad Valmiki Ramayana*, Vol. 1, eds T.R. Krishnacharya and T.K. Venkobacharya, Madras, 1929.
162. Ed. M. Hang, Bombay, 1863.
163. Fig wood.
164. Ed. V. Fausboll, London (undated).
165. Told of in *Pre-Buddhist India*, Ratilal Mehta, Bombay, 1943.
166. Anointing.
167. Ed. P.C. Roy.
168. *Edicts of Asoka Priyadarsin*—trs. Murti and Aiyangar, 1950.
169. R.N. Salatore, *Life in the Gupta Age*, Bombay, 1943.
170. The Buddha, his teachings and the Order of the Monks. In these three does the Buddhist worshipper find refuge.
171. In his *A History of Ceylon for Schools* (Colombo 1945) Fr S.G. Perera states: 'At the beginning of the 16th century, the island was politically divided into three chief kingdoms: Kotte, Jaffna and Kandy, and a number of lesser states. The kingdom of Kotte was the richest, the largest in size and the greatest in

power. It consisted of the south-west portion of the island, from the central hills to the sea... (it) was divided into the provinces of the Seven Korales, the Four Korales, the Three Korales, the Two Korales (or Denavaka), Rayigama and Matara, each of which were governed by a ruler... The king of Kotte...claimed imperial rights over the rest of the island, and was called the Chakravarti, 'Overlord' or Emperor of Lanka. Once a year, each sub-king or prince or ruler of state came to Kotte with his retinue and tribute for the *Perahera* or muster of the states. This Perahera was held on 16 successive nights and the failure to attend the Perahera was punished by war... Sitawaka of old was a venerable kingdom, sweeping from the foothills to the close proximity of Kotte. Chilaw lay on the west coast, northwards of Colombo; Batticaloa is on the east coast and Yala was part of the old kingdom of Ruhuna.'

172. In the old eastern Uva province.

173. The Two Korales of old.

174. Queyroz, *Temporal & Spiritual Conquest of Ceylon*.

175. Trincomalee today.

176. The pilgrim path from Trincomalee to Kataragama. 'Pada' meaning 'feet' for the pilgrimage was always conducted on foot.

177. A Buddha to be.

178. Hugh Nevil, *Sinhala Verse*, ed. P.E.P. Deraniyagala, Ceylon National Museum Manuscript Series, Vol. I, Colombo, 1954.

179. Flower altar.

180. According to Hindu and local belief, Pattini approached with tinkling bangles. The light that is said to hover around the one she favours is the light of her ear jewel, and she comes in the forms of the seven Pattini goddesses and surrounded by the Kadavara gods. Her breasts are covered with garlands of flowers and there is always the smell of ripe mangoes about her, since her seventh self was born in a mango.

181. This great rock, Dimbulagala, as already told of in *Children of the Lion* (Ch. 19, 'The Triumph of Pandukabhaya') is where Panduk Abhaya gathered his troops to fight his uncles.
182. This village still stands at the 174th milepost on the Tissa-Maharama-Wellawaya road. It is called Ranawaranagama today. The old name Oyagama was previously Oyagawa (Sinhala: 'near the Oya') since it rose near the Kirindi Oya.
183. Ebony.
184. This is a special limestone used to good effect by sculptors of old. The stone, when cut, appears to diffuse rays of colour when the sun falls on it.
185. The jungle robin, or Shama.
186. The white-browed fantail flycatcher.
187. *Mimusops hexandra.* Tannin is obtained from the bark of this tree which is a native of India and Sri Lanka.
188. *Vitex altissima.* Also a native of India and Sri Lanka, this tree yields both timber and cabinet wood.
189. *Schleichera trijuga,* the macassar oil tree.
190. *Dimophandra mora.* Noted for its excellent timber and immense seed.
191. *Bassia longifolia.* An oil-yielding tree favoured by bees for its honey-flowers. The flowers are dried and eaten. In India, the fleshy flowers of both the mi and the butter tree (*Bassia latifolia*) are gathered by poor villagers to be dried and eaten. Each tree is said to produce about 200 pounds of flowers in the month of February.
192. In old times, these stone slabs were symbols of worship, before the making of the Buddha image.
193. Songs sung in the form of a competitive dialogue.
194. Watch huts from where the villagers guarded their crops.
195. Threshing floors.
196. Four-lined stanzas.

197. The god Ganesh.
198. The rock of the sun.
199. Thalay or thalé—a blade.
200. Sinhala: 'Giant's hearth'.
201. *Jataka*, ed. V. Fausball, London.
202. Royal sword.
203. White umbrella.
204. Forehead band.
205. Yaktail fan.
206. Royal golden slippers.
207. Umbrella.
208. A single strand of pearls that the king will wear.
209. Heir to the throne.
210. Heir apparent.
211. Turban.
212. The sacred thread.
213. *Persea semecarpifolia*—a much branched tree common in the dry region.
214. The open courtyard around the bo tree.
215. An aeon which consists of a thousand colossal cycles of time, or *maha yuga*. Each kalpa is divided into four yugas or ages—Krta, Treta, Dvapara and Kali. At the end of each kalpa comes a cosmic dissolution or *kalpa vinasa,* caused by such different agencies as wind, water and fire.
216. These lines are from *Morte d'Arthur,* written by Tennyson in 1835. Readers will understand why we have employed the Tennysonian device to tell of the passing of Vihara Maha Devi. Surprisingly, no historical chronicle or the literature of Lanka gives any account of her death, undoubtedly the greatest queen of all and mother of a hero king. We remind, however, that ancient tradition upholds that Vihara Maha Devi will return some day, when the country needs her most. This is very much like the Arthurian legend. We trust that such taking of historical liberties will not be found too offensive.